There's a
Pair of Us

JULIENE ANNE

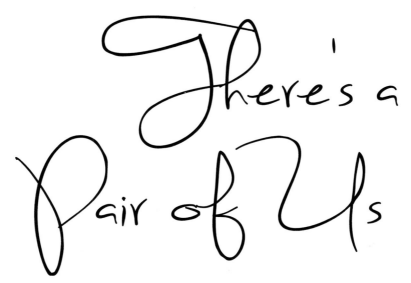

There's a Pair of Us

A Memoir of a Marriage

TATE PUBLISHING
AND ENTERPRISES, LLC

Published by Tate Publishing & Enterprises, LLC
127 E. Trade Center Terrace | Mustang, Oklahoma 73064 USA
1.888.361.9473 | www.tatepublishing.com

Tate Publishing is committed to excellence in the publishing industry. The company reflects the philosophy established by the founders, based on Psalm 68:11,
"The Lord gave the word and great was the company of those who published it."

Published in the United States of America

ISBN: 978-1-62295-001-0
1. Biography & Autobiography / Personal Memoirs
2. Family & Relationships / Marriage
13.01.14

The names and places have been changed to protect the innocent as well as the guilty.

Dedication

For JC, who accepts me regardless, loves me unconditionally, and never lets me down.

Most people are about as happy as they make their minds up to be.

—Abraham Lincoln

Happiness is a choice. Or is it?

Throughout our lives, we are presented with challenges and situations that can make happiness seemingly impossible, but then at the same time we are presented with an opportunity to turn away from our despair and become stronger, wiser and potentially happier. Looking back, I don't think I assumed power over my own contentment until the day my marriage died and God called me to become someone new, someone stronger, someone who could potentially resurrect a marriage and claim power over my own peace and joy.

I would start by detailing the events of that day —the day of anger, punches, and pennies—but that would be moving too fast for you to grasp the clear picture of who I was and who we were before we were forced to look at ourselves, before we questioned whether happiness was a choice we could make and whether we could choose it together.

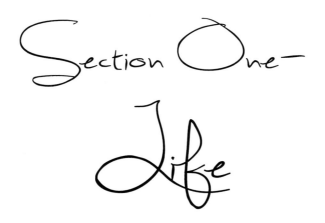

Section One—

Life

CHAPTER

One

"So, do you wanna get married?" he asked me, as casually as though we were talking about whether I wanted to grab a cheeseburger for lunch.

As a girl in my early teens, I used to lie in bed, watching the Labor Day Telethon and imagining my husband lying beside me. Snuggling up to the pillow, content and naïve, I dreamt of the perfect happiness that marriage would bring without considering the possibility that there would be times when I would cry myself dry in the fetal position on the floor of my walk-in closet, times when I would curse aloud, slamming my hand against the steering wheel.

I also had not considered how the proposal would come. Had I thought about it, I'm sure I would have imagined more romance and less of the nausea that accompanied my morning sickness. I was grateful for his apparent sincerity, although I was fairly certain that he was as upset about the turn our lives had taken as I was. But my response probably reflected the sadness and disappointment that overwhelmed me. This was not the way I wanted to wrap myself around his second to last finger. It was September 1985. Lee and I were facing one another in one of the laundromats at

Northeast Missouri State University in Kirksville, Missouri. My clothes had begun their wash cycle only moments before, giving us time to talk, but we were silent, lost in our conflicted feelings and the hypnotic noise of the washers and dryers surrounding us. A woman was folding a white shirt; a man was getting change to start his basketful of laundry—ordinary people going about their ordinary lives while ours were changing forever. It would be years before we'd know if they were changing for better or for worse.

"Are you sure you wanna do this?" I asked, leaning forward in the hard plastic chair.

"You're my snugglie pooh," he told me, his right leg bouncing spastically as he reached over and rubbed my knee.

Grateful for his optimism, I reached out and took his hand, determined that somehow we would make it through whatever lay ahead.

❧

We had met the previous fall, during my freshman year, just after I had broken off a four-year relationship with my high school sweetheart. It was exciting to meet new people, and I was pleasantly surprised to find that a few members of the opposite sex were showing interest in me.

Initially, Lee hadn't noticed me. A good many girls attended the powder puff football practice, and I was not the only one who found his blond good looks desirable as he threw long passes and demonstrated how to run the plays. He also exhibited patience and good humor as twenty-five females ran around the field with hardly a clue as to what they were supposed to be doing.

Given the fact that he was a charming, popular senior, I figured that he was out of my league, but that didn't keep me from hoping, nor did it keep me from engaging in behaviors that might get me noticed. I would position myself in front of him and bend over to snap the ball. I would feign injuries so that he would have to come and check on me. If a pass were thrown fifty feet in front of me, I would dive forward in my white sweatpants and pink T-shirt and skid across the grass-covered field, body outstretched, as if I thought I had a chance at catching the ball. The last tactic brought a smile to his face, and that smile with the single dimple on his left cheek solidified my desire to make him mine.

I don't know if it was my football antics, my persistence, or divine intervention, but something caused him to call me on a Tuesday at midnight and ask if I wanted to have lunch with him at Centennial Hall the next day.

"Sure," I said as nonchalantly as possible, although, after hanging up, I joined my roommates in jumping up and down on our beds.

They were thrilled for me. *I* was thrilled for me.

The next afternoon, I was rendered speechless upon seeing him. He was wearing flip-flops, white painter's paints, and a long-sleeved turquoise T-shirt with a backpack slung over one shoulder.

"I rode my bike," he said with a slightly nervous laugh and a big grin. "The seat was soaked from the rain last night, so my pants are a little wet."

I laughed with him, probably a little too wildly, but the fact that he admitted to his wet bottom made him even more adorable to me. I suppose he had correctly anticipated that I might check out his backside if given the opportunity.

When he said, a little too formally, "Shall we go to lunch?" I giggled and slipped out into the hallway to join him.

After taking our pizzas to a table in the cafeteria, he told me that once, when he had come here wearing white pants, he had lost his grip on his tray and covered himself with sour cream and salsa.

"Did anyone notice?" I asked him, laughing.

"Oh, yeah," he told me. "Everyone in the place gave me a standing O."

He seemed to have an unlimited number of entertaining stories about his life at college, and I listened adoringly, thinking of how mundane my life had been until now and amazed that, for some reason that I could not understand, he seemed to be as enamored with me as I was with him.

On that mild, fall day with college students bustling all around us and the scent of burgers, chicken, and lasagna in the air, feeling happy with Lee was like blinking: it happened without thought or effort. In that moment, so early in our relationship—he with pizza sauce on the corner of his mouth and me with teeth not yet straightened by braces—neither of us could have ever imagined what the years ahead would bring. It's best that way.

"How about going for a walk with me tomorrow night?" he asked as we were finishing. "I could show you around the downtown and some of the popular hangouts."

"That'd be nice," I replied, when what I really wanted to say was, "Heck, yeah!"

The next evening, a little after the sun had set, he knocked on my dorm room door again, this time wearing blue jeans and a big sweatshirt. After introducing him to my roommates who were standing in the center of the room, grinning at us, we took the stairs to the first floor and out into the fresh night air.

"So, you're turning the big nineteen, huh?" he said later (in the course of our conversation, I mentioned that my birthday was coming up). And when I explained that I was only seventeen, he turned so reflective that I could only hope he didn't feel the three-and-a-half-year age difference was too great. We walked in silence for a couple of minutes, and then he let it go, and we were talking comfortably again. I would come to appreciate, envy, and occasionally curse that ability of his to let issues drop and not worry about them anymore.

We walked around the town square and city hall, passing Pagliai's Pizza, which would become one of our favorite places to share a Ronza, and the jewelers where one year later, I would be picking out a wedding ring. We talked about our majors, his in industrial technology and mine in math education, as well as our childhoods. The youngest of six, I had been raised a Catholic in a city in Illinois, and he was a nonpracticing Methodist, raised on a farm in Iowa, the oldest of three, both of us from lower-middle class families. I remembered that I had heard in one of my psychology classes that firstborn/lastborn marriage combinations had the greatest chance of success, but I decided not to raise that particular subject at that early stage of our relationship.

By the time we stood at the steps to my dormitory, we knew a great deal about one another, and our attraction had not appeared to wane. Months later I would learn that, when he went back to his apartment, he had called his best friend and told him that he had met the girl he was going to marry.

&

Someone put coins in a nearby dryer.

"I could call Planned Parenthood and see how much an abortion would cost," I said.

"Okay," he replied. "But only if you want to."

He had to know I didn't want to do any such thing. I had told him before that I was opposed to abortion, and I hadn't even been willing to take birth control, because it was against my beliefs. Too bad I hadn't been as staunch in my stance against premarital sex. By offering to call, I was merely trying to show a willingness to look at other possibilities, and I suppose I was testing him and his true feelings about marrying me. He didn't pass, but I wasn't surprised. Friends had previously joked that I was only in college to get my MRS degree, and to be fair, I knew that I believed in the *happily ever after* more than he did.

I made the call, but they wouldn't give me the information without an appointment, and I didn't want that. So it was settled. We would marry in a month and a half.

CHAPTER

Two

I had my concerns about getting married. They went beyond the obvious—our ages, our poverty, our religious differences, and the fact that we were marrying more out of obligation than desire. Lee was extremely outgoing, which also translated into him being flirtatious. He loved being the center of attention, which meant that he was occasionally annoying to me in his attempts to entertain other people, especially women. He was usually the life of the party and occasionally drank too much. Bottom line— he was funny, lighthearted, unrestrained, and a good time. These issues caused me to question whether marrying him was a good idea, but, ironically enough, they were also the same reasons I was attracted to him. While he viewed life as an opportunity to have fun, I took everything more seriously. I wanted to be amused and enjoy myself, but not at the expense of being reckless or immoral, particularly since I was working on getting a front-row ticket to the concert of heaven where Jesus would be the opening act and God the headliner. I wanted to live for the next life. He didn't seem convinced there was one. I ignored the unrest that his lack of religion caused me.

Early in the relationship, I learned that he didn't make responsible decisions on a consistent basis. Once when he came to pick me up sporting a fat lip and a bruised face, his explanation was that he had been drinking the night before and had put his car in a ditch after jumping a driveway near his home. His casual attitude made it clear he didn't see it as the big deal that I thought it was. We hadn't yet gotten to a place where I was comfortable voicing my true feelings about serious issues. I was far too infatuated to criticize him at that point.

On another occasion, I had been thinking about and regretting the fact that I had had sex with my ex-boyfriend, and I asked him if he had had sex with anyone other than his long-term girlfriend, he, unruffled, replied, "Yeah," and I was completely taken aback. I'm not sure what prompted the question. Until that moment, I had believed when we had intercourse, it would be special for both of us. I thought we both envisioned it as behavior reserved exclusively for committed relationships, but his indifference did more than challenge that belief; it negated it. I replayed his response in my mind over and over, in the hopes of finding some air of regret in his tone or his expression, but I couldn't find any. The easy response told me that I didn't want to ask how many others he had slept with, because I would not have been pleased.

I did not question him further. In fact, I didn't speak to him again for about a day and a half. I had to process that new information and figure out how it fit into us, if there was going to be an *us*. I had to decide how important his sexual history was to me. And it wasn't only about his history; it was about his attitude. My ex and I had only been with one another. And we had taken it very seriously. In fact, we had had sex only a few times in the three years we were together, and we had gone to confession afterward. For Lee, seeking mutual forgiveness from a higher power would have been laughable.

Despite my Goody-two-shoes attitude and his promiscuous ways, I stayed in the relationship, probably because the list of pros—topped by the facts that he was spontaneous, surprising, and entertaining—was longer than the list of cons. Dates were often unusual, including, the Saturday morning when he whisked me away to Pancake Days in Centerville, Iowa, where we shared a record number of pancakes and our first syrupy, sticky kiss, which he described as a hard peck that needed some practice. And once he turned up outside my second-floor dorm room window and shouted, "Rapunzel, Rapunzel, let down your golden red hair and let me come up."

Another time we took Kentucky Fried Chicken to Thousand Hills State Park and shared a picnic and a cartwheel competition. His cartwheels were little more than putting his hands on the ground and lifting his feet about five inches while my performance was so superior that he was forced to concede, reluctantly awarding me with his little bucket dessert, from which I fed him spoonfuls as we lay on a blanket, alternating between studying and making out. I remember reciting from my favorite poet, Emily Dickinson:

> I'm nobody! Who are you?
> Are you nobody, too?
> Then there's a pair of us — don't tell!
> They'd banish us, you know.
> How dreary to be somebody!
> How public, like a frog
> To tell your name the livelong day
> To an admiring bog!

"I like that," he said, kissing me. "'I'm nobody! Who are you?' That's going to be our poem from now on."

And many nights, back at his apartment, we snuggled on the couch and watched David Letterman until it seemed too late for me to return to my dorm room. On more days than we should have, we ditched classes to sneak away to Dairy Queen for a Peanut Buster Parfait. And if we happened not to be together and he spotted me across the quad, he would yell, "Miss Juliene," and I would run and jump into his open arms. We wanted to spend every moment together, and the falling star that we saw after our first real date on September 28, 1984, was an indication to both of us that being together was the way it was meant to be.

I did, however, break up with him once. When I chose not to go to a university basketball game in February, Lee went with a couple of friends. Afterward, without telling me, he had a party in his room, and when I met him for lunch the next day, he was sporting dark circles under his eyes and a newly pierced ear.

"Where did you get that?" I asked.

"Things got a little crazy last night."

"Really," I replied. Not being a fan of men with pierced ears, especially when the piercing was the result of late night drinking and partying, I wasn't sure what else to say.

"This girl said she could do it for me," he explained, "so we went into the bathroom, and she put an ice cube behind my ear. When she jabbed me with her earring, I passed out. I think I must have hit the sink," he added, rubbing his head. "Kinda crazy, huh?"

We were walking down the narrow dormitory hallway on our way to the cafeteria. I stared ahead and, occasionally, our elbows bumped, which caused me to grit my teeth. I felt what he had done was wrong on numerous levels. First of all, he had had people, girls in particular, at his apartment, and he had not let me know about it. Secondly, he had been in his bathroom with a female that I was not familiar with, and he had let her pierce his ear with her own earring. And third, to further emphasize his weakness as a human being, he had passed out. I was disgusted with him.

Nearly twenty-five years later, I look back on that day and wonder why I made up with him. Clearly we were in two different places with regards to acceptable behavior. But, at the time, enamored as I was with Lee, I was convinced that he was my destiny.

So, regardless of my concerns, we married.

CHAPTER
Three

For a hurry-up, no money wedding, it was nice. Before moving me back home from college, Lee bought a five-hundred-dollar wedding ring that I had picked out at the downtown Kirksville jewelry store. He had enough money in his savings to get the ring and put a few hundred dollars toward the wedding, but he was working a temporary job for six dollars an hour, so the cash flow was minimal and not stable. I hoped to get a job after the wedding and before the baby came, but I was unsure of what I would be able to find in Lee's small hometown of Fort Madison, where we had rented a house. Our families were unable to give much financial assistance.

One of his aunts found a wedding dress at a garage sale. It fit well, and the fact that it wasn't completely hideous was a bonus. Another of his aunts made our flowers. One of Lee's friends sang, and another took our pictures. We found a cheap reception hall and disc jockey, and my maid of honor and sister-in-law stayed up late with me the night before the wedding, making sandwiches for the reception. Instead of being dizzy with excitement about the great day ahead, all I could focus on was layering bread, ham, cheese, and another slice of bread. Cut from one end to the other, and then do it all again, and again, and again.

Thankfully my hometown priest was willing to waive the six-month advance notice typically expected by the church and only one of us had to be Catholic to be married there. We had over three hundred guests, and other than my ex-boyfriend, everyone seemed happy for us and hopeful, even though I'm sure they had their doubts about our future as man and wife. They weren't the only ones with doubts. Just before leaving the dressing room to walk down the aisle of the large Roman Catholic Church, I gave in to a fit of tears. My mother looked at me with alarm as if she thought I might dart out the nearest exit.

"What's wrong?" she asked.

I wanted to say, "Well, I'm nineteen years old, pregnant, and about to get married to a man with questionable values and problematic behaviors," but I refrained. She did not deserve to be the brunt of my sarcasm.

"I'll be fine," was all I said.

As I walked down the aisle, Lee greeted me at the altar with a convincing enough smile, but once we were face-to-face with the priest, he seemed to be taking such deep breaths that it occurred to me that he was trying to inhale enough oxygen to remain upright.

It was a fairly lengthy, late, Saturday afternoon Catholic mass, complete with Communion, but even though it was long, I'm short on memories. I do not recall saying my vows on that day. Since then, I have had reason to call them into question on numerous occasions. *Did I really say, "For better or worse?" And did I mean it? Did I even understand what I was saying?* Anyway, I'll get back to that later.

The reception was much like the wedding: a blur of the friendly faces of smiling people who were secretly thanking God they weren't us. Some well-wishes seemed like condolences as friends reminded me that I had been such a good student and that they were sad to go back to the university without me. They seemed to think it was the end of the line for me as far as a degree and career were concerned. Fortunately, because of my confidence in my own abilities, I did not share their concerns.

By the time we left the reception, we were both exhausted, and I was actually feeling faint, no doubt because the growing fetus inside me had not gotten enough nourishment throughout that busy day and neither had I. Still wearing his tuxedo, Lee's brother drove us home on roads that had been lightly dusted with snow. We made a stop at a Hardee's drive-thru window, where I was provided nourishment in the form of a hot ham and cheese as well as fries, which I shared with Lee. As far as I was concerned, it was a fine way to begin a marriage.

The fact that we were both unpretentious boded well for the honeymoon, which featured a two-night stay at a hotel called the Pzazz in Burlington, Iowa. The room had a king-size bed and heart-shaped hot tub and was nicer than anything either of us had ever stayed in before. We threw all the money from the dollar dance onto that big ol' bed and rolled around on it. Seventy-five George Washingtons had never had so much fun. At that delirious moment, it was easy to believe that we were going to be happy ever after.

But the next morning, I awoke to reality. I was unsure of myself, unsure of my ability to please this person for the rest of our lives. Lee, apparently unbothered by any doubts, milled about the room, eating cold pizza, reading the sports section, and making idle conversation about the Hawkeyes having beaten Purdue. When he suggested that we go for a swim in the indoor pool just beyond the sliding doors, and I replied that we'd have to be careful to keep the doors shut or the dehumidifier in our room might suck all the water out of the pool, he cracked up. Even though it was a corny joke, I appreciated that laugh more than he knew, because all the awkwardness I was feeling dissolved. Wrapping my arms around him, I suggested that we enjoy the privacy of our hot tub.

When our brief vacation was over, we returned to the home where we would live together as man and wife—a century-old, rundown farmhouse set smack dab in the middle of cornfields, for which we paid $125 a month. In the bigger of the two small bedrooms, we had placed a mattress and box springs, which left just enough room for an old chest of drawers. The other bedroom would eventually house a crib and changing table. We were given a worn green couch, a brown recliner, and a nineteen-inch black and white television. Those three items filled the living room. In the kitchen, the owners had left a round, metal table and two chairs with torn plastic seats. Thank goodness I had not been raised a fancy girl. On our third day of marriage, as Lee left for work in our only vehicle, a 1972 Plymouth Fury that required a screwdriver stuck somewhere under the hood to start, I threw myself on that makeshift bed and cried.

I was not able to choose happiness at that time.

In fact, the thought had not even occurred to me.

CHAPTER

Four

Happiness was not completely nonexistent in that home, however.

"Meeery Chriiistmaaas," Lee boomed in his best and deepest Santa voice as he came in the door, wearing a Santa hat and bearing an armful of gifts.

I was thrilled to see him. He was just getting home from working the overnight shift, and I had spent Christmas Eve alone.

"Look what Santa brought you, little girl," he went on, grinning proudly.

"Santa didn't think I was too naughty, huh?" I asked him.

"Ohhh nooo, Santa wants you to be even naughtier. Santa likes when you're a bad girl," he assured me, putting down the presents and holding out his arms. "Come show Santa how naughty you can be."

I enjoyed being playful, but my ever-growing belly was not exactly putting me in the mood to be a naughty girl. Lee thought my changing figure was awesome, so his sex drive was not diminishing. He had come up with the idea of putting a penny in a jar every time we made love during the first year of our marriage and taking one out every time we had sex after that to prove his theory that we would make love more often in that first year than all the rest of our married life. It sounded to me like an attempt to have an inordinate amount of sex before our first anniversary, and had I not been pregnant, I might have been more enthused about his plan.

That first Christmas as a married couple was as good as it could be for two impoverished, young people expecting an unplanned baby. Certainly, we both began the New Year in a hopeful frame of mind.

Lee had applied for a full-time job with the company where his dad worked, and on January 21, when the long awaited call finally came, all I could do was hug my midsection and thank God.

When he hung up, we danced around the kitchen in one another's arms, singing, "We got some monnnney, nahna, nahna, nahna, na," as though we had won the lottery. And for us, that was exactly what it was. Lee would make $21,000 a year, and we would have insurance for the baby's birth. He had gotten a real job, one that would save us financially.

I, on the other hand, had been turned down when I had applied as a checkout girl at the Aldi Food Store. To save myself further humiliation, we decided I should stay home until after the baby was born. I don't think I was depressed during that time, but I remember sleeping quite a bit, watching a lot of soap operas, and eating whatever I could find. Occasionally I would think of my friends at college with envy. But then I would remember that college for me had become completely about Lee, and I would convince myself that I was where I was supposed to be, which was easy on the days that Lee came home from work and we watched *The Wheel of Fortune* and *The Newlywed Game* and then played Yahtzee. But more often than not, he came in the door and reported that his dad needed help building a fence, working on a car, or plowing a field. Now that we lived only a few miles down the road from his parents, his presence seemed to be constantly required. I'm not sure how the farm survived while Lee was at college.

I resented the times that he left me to go help his dad, but I did not resent them as much as I did when the weekend came and he wanted to go out with his brother or best friend. My friends and family were in another city, in another state, and I didn't want to spend more time alone.

"We'll just go out for a little while," he'd say, and even though I knew a little while would mean several hours, I usually wouldn't or couldn't convince him to stay home. When he came home, I would pout, and when he apologized, I would pout some more until he promised to change his ways and I would forgive him. Thus began our pattern of ineffective marital communication.

CHAPTER

Five

Three weeks before the due date, and having prepared ourselves with only one Lamaze class, I called Lee at work and told him I was spotting.

"What does that mean?" he demanded, clearly concerned.

"It means that we're going to have the baby sooner than we thought," I told him impatiently. "At least that's what I think. I'm going to see the doctor at four."

"You're going to make an awesome momma," he told me, and although I appreciated his confidence in me, that moment was the first time I truly considered the implications of what was about to happen. I was nineteen and about to experience childbirth, soon to have a baby that would need me every day, all day. I wasn't prepared for childbirth, nor was I prepared to be a mother, but nature didn't care.

The doctor confirmed what I had assumed. I would need to enter the hospital and remain there until the baby was born, which he believed should be within the next twenty-four hours. I packed a small bag, and we loaded it in the car with a car seat and blanket for the baby. Lee's new job had allowed us to get a new car that had working seatbelts, and as an added benefit, it could be started by simply turning a key in the ignition. He drove me from our little country house into the small town hospital, chatting nervously while I sat in thoughtful silence, watching the open fields gradually give way to sparse and insignificant houses and businesses.

I think I grunted, "I don't know," several times as he interrupted my silence with questions such as, "What time do you think the baby will be born? Do you think it's a boy or a girl? How big do you think the baby will be?" I knew he was excited, but I also knew that soon my quiet moments would be interrupted by the cries of a newborn.

When the hospital came into view, I was thankful, although I had yet to experience any other signs that would lead me to believe I would give birth anytime soon. As I lifted my basketball-size belly from the car and felt the cool spring air on my face, I felt hopeful. It was the season of birth and of promises fulfilled, and I was certain that everything was going to be fine. But, as we entered the hospital, I found myself becoming anxious. People came here because they needed help. I didn't want to need help. I didn't want the glances of the nurses and doctors who would judge us, because of our youth, and condemn our baby's future. But, at this point, there was no alternative.

We were taken to the maternity ward where I continued to be reflective as I went to the bathroom and took off my worn white sneakers, black cotton pants with the stretchable waist, and my oversized T-shirt, and slipped into a singularly unattractive hospital gown, climbed into bed, and attempted to relax. Lee, however, was not a model of relaxation. During times of stress or excitement, he demonstrated convincing symptoms of attention-deficit/hyperactivity disorder. Some part of his body was in constant motion, whether he was pacing the room, bouncing his knee up and down, or mouthing one question after another. "What should I do? Is there anything I should be doing? What do you want me to do?"

Our second Lamaze class was taking place that evening in the hospital, so I sent him to tell the teacher why we were absent, but it was actually to give myself fifteen minutes of peace and quiet before he returned to happily announce that he had shared with the teacher and other soon-to-be parents that we were so good we were graduating early.

The contractions started shortly thereafter. I hadn't experienced much physical pain in my life, so I was not sure what to expect. Initially, they were bearable and spaced fairly far apart. But after a few hours, as the time approached midnight, they were becoming more bothersome. When he wasn't being too hyper, Lee was great. He held my hand and looked at his watch. Then he would refer to the handouts that we had received at our Lamaze class.

"I'm thinking you are probably dilated to a seven or eight, based on the spacing of your contractions," he pointed out.

I knew that once I made it to ten, the baby would be born.

"Oh, thank goodness!" I exclaimed. "It would be wonderful if the baby wants to come out sometime soon."

At that point, the nurse entered the room.

"Things are moving right along," I told her proudly. "The contractions are getting harder and closer together."

"Sounds good," she said. "Let's check you out and see where you're at."

She laid the bed flat, asked me to bend my knees with legs apart, and then put her gloved hand under my gown. It seemed a crude way to gain a measurement and not at all scientific, but she seemed certain about her conclusion when she said, "You're almost dilated two centimeters."

I thought she was kidding, but there was no sign that she was trying to be amusing as she checked my vital signs. I settled in for what was to be a long night.

Lee had remained at my side throughout most of it, dozing occasionally or flipping channels on the television. I had rubbed the back of his hand between the contractions and squeezed his thumb during them. When I finally said, "I don't know how much more of this I can take," he became so nervous that I shouted, "I'm not going to die! I just want this to be over!"

He was still looking at me with fear in his eyes when the nurse entered the room to check me for the umpteenth time. Actually, she was the third nurse, because the shift had changed twice since I arrived. I had been pleasant toward the earlier nurses, but by this point, I had lost my tolerance for the slow progression of the dilation that each one reported to me. Without a word to her, I bent my knees, spread my legs, and tore back the covers so she could do her job.

"You're dilated between an eight and eight and a half," she said, her voice giving the impression she was pleased with me.

"Great," I wailed. "At this rate, I should be dilated ten in about another dozen hours."

Then another contraction hit, as if to punish me for being sarcastic, and I firmly placed my head on the pillow, closed my eyes, and tried to concentrate on the Lamaze breathing technique that had thus far given me little relief.

"Hee-hee-hoooo, hee-hee-hoooo, hee-hee-hoooo."

Was I supposed to breathe in on the hees and out on the hoos or the other way around? Or maybe I was supposed to breathe out on all of them and then in on the next group? I began to feel dizzy, no doubt because I was doing it too quickly, but I was still clear-headed enough to realize prayer would likely be the better strategy, so I prayed, a simple prayer.

God, please help me to get through this. Let this baby be healthy, and get it out of me soon. Please, God.

I don't know if two hours would be considered soon, but by ten that morning, I was finally fully dilated and was being wheeled to the delivery room, where my doctor was waiting for me. I was relieved to see him and comforted by the fact that he had plenty of experience, nearly twenty-three years earlier he had delivered Lee.

I was transferred to the delivery table, and my feet were placed in the cold, hard stirrups. When the next contraction came and I was invited to push, I was eager to cooperate. Although Lee was standing close by, I paid no attention to him, since my sole purpose at this point was to give birth and end this pain until, that is, I heard the nurse ask him if he was okay, and I saw him, bent over from the waist with his hands on his knees, claiming to be lightheaded.

I tried not to lose my concentration, but I was thinking, *Are you kidding me? Can I not even be the center of attention when I am giving birth?*

Somehow I stayed the course, however, and at eleven minutes after ten, the doctor said, "It's a girl."

CHAPTER

$\mathcal{S}$ix

Lee and I were amazed that we had accidentally created this incredible little human. Nicole appeared to be perfect with her ten fingers and ten toes and flawless skin; however, she was not a good sleeper. Lee worked rotating shifts, so I dreaded the weeks that he worked overnight when, awakened every two hours by her hunger cries, I took her from the used bassinette that we had been given and sat up in bed, resting against the wall, drowsily nursing her back to sleep. All too often I was disturbed by the sound of what seemed to be a multitude of mice scratching at the ceiling, as well as contemplating the dangers that might be present outside in the cornfields. I prayed to God, and I prayed to the clock, trying to force the numbers on the digital screen to read seven-thirty, when the sound of gravel crunching under the tires of the car would bring relief from the terrors of the night and I would hear Lee call out, "Good morning, sunshine. How are my ladies?"

Curled up under the covers with Nicole snuggled against my breast, I loved it when Lee bent down and kissed her forehead, her eyelids fluttering and her lips sucking air as though she were still eating. Then, when he had showered and slid in next to me, I could finally sleep soundly until hunger would awaken the baby once again, and she and I would begin our day.

When I planned to have her baptized into the Catholic faith, no one questioned it. Lee was attending mass with me occasionally and was content to allow me to raise her and any future children we might have as Catholics. We invited both our families to our home and threw an outdoor party after the ceremony at the church. During the previous week, I had planned food for forty and had furiously cleaned that small house. Lee had worked on the yard, and, although some of the guests may have thought our home was shabby, we were proud. We were a team while we were preparing for the reception, but the night before the baptism some cracks appeared in our united front.

A family friend had invited us to a party. We found a sitter for Nicole and decided to go for only a short while, or so I thought. Unlike Lee, I knew very few of the guests, and I was bored and tired by eleven, not to mention being disgusted by the amount of alcohol being consumed by my husband. But when I suggested that we leave, he told me to go ahead and take the car and go home alone.

I was overwhelmed by negative emotions. I wanted to say or do something that would change the situation, but I had learned from past experience that moments such as this had no solution or positive outcome. When I held out my hand for the keys, he reached in his pocket and gave them to me without establishing eye contact, and I knew there was no chance he would change his mind.

At five in the morning, he finally came home, got into bed, and promptly fell asleep, leaving me awake and furious, as I had been most of the night, until Nicole began to cry.

"Are you excited about the big day?" I asked her, taking her out of her crib. "Mommy's excited that you are being baptized but not so excited about the day. I'm exhausted before it has even begun, and I'm not at all happy with your father."

And because she looked at me as though she understood every word, I continued to vent as I changed her and put on her christening gown. I dressed myself as noisily as possible until Lee finally stirred and squinted at me with one eye.

"Oh, I'm sorry. Did I wake you?" I asked, my voice both sugar and spice.

"No, I just happened to wake up," he responded groggily.

We didn't speak again for the next eight hours, although we stood side by side, smiling at our guests at the baptismal ceremony. After the reception, we cleaned up in silence. I was extremely relieved when the last family member left and the last dish was washed, but I was left with nothing to think about but my anger. I waited patiently for him to say something, anything, so I could pounce. We were in our bedroom getting ready to go to bed when he finally spoke.

"I'm sorry about staying out so late and drinking so much."

"Screw you!" I replied. "You knew we had this party today and it was a special day for Nicole, and you didn't even care. You knew I wanted you to leave with me, and again you didn't care. You are selfish and inconsiderate, and I'm tired of you and your crap."

"Look," he said, "it's not that big of a deal. I got up and helped out all day today, so settle down."

He had chosen the epitome of responses guaranteed to make the situation worse.

"I won't settle down!" I shouted. "And I hate it when you tell me to. I'm sick and tired of you trying to wiggle out of taking responsibility for your bad behavior, and I hate this marriage!"

Grabbing a suitcase from the closet, I heaved it at him. The impact was minimal, but his eyes became huge with surprise as he took in the full force of my anger.

"Why don't you leave for a while?" I screamed. "Obviously you don't care about being in this marriage or acting like a husband or father."

"I think you're overreacting," he told me, rolling his eyes.

This reaction was number two on the list of responses that exacerbated the situation.

"I'm not overreacting," I told him. "You're underreacting, and you have yet to explain to me where you were until five in the morning. Do you think it is okay that you did that? I lay awake half the night, worrying."

"No, I don't think it's okay," he replied. "I said I'm sorry. I fell asleep in the backseat of Joe's car and ended up at his house. I didn't mean for that to happen. And I came home as soon as I woke up."

I looked into his eyes and searched his face for traces of dishonesty. But the fact that I didn't see any, didn't prove innocence. Regardless of where he ended up, the situation was wrong, and it was going to take me some time to move on.

CHAPTER

Seven

As the end of the summer of 1986 approached, our lives were improving. Lee's salary increased to the point that we no longer qualified for food stamps, and the lady from the WIC (Women, Infants, and Children) Program didn't visit as regularly. I'm not positive, but I think her purpose was to ensure that all the strikes against us weren't going to cause Nicole to be developmentally delayed. I felt both offended and proud when she paid us a visit. Nicole was amazingly on track at three months, and because of that, I looked forward to showing off her ability to lift her own three-pound head, smile, and roll from her belly to her back. Despite her parents' lack of preparedness, Nicole was definitely going to be a wonderful and brilliant child.

Other pluses occurred as well. Lee's grandmother loaned us $13,000 to buy a twenty-year-old gold trailer with a freestanding, two-stall garage on a one-acre lot, which, although outside the city limits, meant that I had neighbors nearby and could feel more relaxed when Lee wasn't home. We also decided that I should return to school.

"Are you sure we can afford to have me taking classes again?" I asked. "We have a car payment, a monthly payment to your grandma, a hospital bill, and we're still paying off the loan from my first year of college."

Since Lee had been a resident assistant during the fall and spring semesters and worked through the summers, he had been able to graduate with minimal debt. Now he was the sole bread winner and paying not only our bills but also any expenses that I incurred such as my previous schooling and any continued education.

"I think we can swing it, since the classes at the community college are cheap," he said, "and you can at least finish your two-year degree. My mom is willing to watch Nicole if you take classes between her bus routes, so we won't be paying for a sitter."

I had always been independent and a hard worker. In fact, I had been given the award for contributing the most to my high school graduating class. Furthermore, I wanted to be able to help share the burden of our expenses.

"I feel guilty that you're taking care of all our bills," I said.

"Well, you know how you can make it up to me," he said, grinning suggestively.

I still hadn't given into the idea of getting on the pill, but I had begun using a diaphragm. I'm not sure why I felt God would be more accepting of that form of birth control, maybe because we weren't always consistent about using it. By January of 1987, I was pregnant again.

How could a girl who was bright enough to be secretary of the National Honor Society be stupid enough to allow a second pregnancy before the age of twenty? Call it stupidity. Call it God's will. Either way, we were about to become parents to a second unplanned baby.

Nicole was nearly a year old before she slept through the night, and as she began walking, she was a challenge to keep up with. She didn't want to go to bed at night, so if we put her in her crib before she was ready, she would kick her legs over the side and slide down the rails and walk herself right out of the bedroom. She got into cabinets, climbed out of her high chair and sat on the tray, and took off her clothes whenever possible. Once, she managed to get into my makeup and grind black mascara into the light peach carpet of the bathroom. Granted, it was an older trailer and not the Taj Mahal, but the bathroom had been done in pleasant colors, and I had liked it until that moment.

I had also liked my child until that moment. I leaned over and grabbed her arm harder than a mother should and screamed louder than a mother should, "No, Nicole, no makeup!" I looked into her eyes, trying to impress my disappointment and anger onto her, but her eyes did not register understanding or caring, just fear. I let go of her arm, and she scampered out of the room, crying.

I leaned my back against the bathroom wall and slid one vertebra at a time down, down, down, until I hit rock bottom. Then, I too began crying. *How,* I wondered, *was I ever going to be able to take care of two children when I seemed to be scarcely able to take care of just one?* Even though I was young, I was exhausted most of the time. No doubt I would be happy again, but just then, being both a mother and a mother-to-be, I couldn't see it happening.

That is, until Nicole peeked at me around the corner and said, "Saw-e, Mommy."

CHAPTER
Eight

When I told Lee it was time to go, I wasn't referring to the Cardinal's Baseball game we had planned to attend.

"Lee," I said, this time a little louder as he made the groaning noises that we all make when unwillingly being aroused from a deep sleep, "it's time to go to the hospital. I've been up since two with contractions, and I think we'd better be leaving now."

Less than eighteen months prior to this day, Lee and I had experienced a childbirth that had been lengthy and laborious, which probably explained why he didn't move with the alacrity that one might expect from a father-to-be.

"Do I have time to take a shower?" he asked, yawning.

I had been up for the past five hours, cleaning the trailer and packing an overnight bag, regularly gripping nearby furniture as the contractions came and went. I knew they were closer together and stronger than they had been even an hour before, but I too had the memory of eighteen months before, and so I told him I guessed it would be okay.

But when he came out of the shower and saw me holding the top of the dresser, bearing down through another contraction, he hurried to dress himself and then Nicole. But when I saw him struggling to put shoes on her, I lost patience.

"We're just taking her to your mother's. I don't think shoes are necessary."

He looked up, startled by my snippiness, and said, "Oh, all right. Let's go then," like someone who was accustomed to my short temper, which, I'm afraid, he was.

When we got to his parents' house, I stayed in the car while he ran Nicole inside. I take that back. He didn't run her inside; he walked, and then he proceeded to have a conversation with his mom or maybe they played a game of Euchre. I'm not sure. I only know he took his time getting back to the car.

When we were back on the road, headed toward the hospital, he asked with the calmness of a man who has nothing on his daily agenda, "Would it be okay if I stop to get some donuts?"

At this time I was leaning forward with my knees apart and bracing myself with a death grip on the dashboard, and when I turned to look at him, he said, "Okay. Maybe we'd better just get to the hospital."

Once I was inside and in a wheelchair, Lee pushed me to the maternity ward. When the nurse handed me a gown, I sensed that she and Lee shared the same attitude when it came to the speed with which they needed to move. Fifteen minutes later, she casually lifted my gown and exclaimed, "Wow! You're dilated ten centimeters. I have to call the doctor. Don't start pushing," before she rushed out of the room.

I gave Lee an *I told you so* look, but it must have escaped him, because he gave me his best and biggest smile and declared, "Good job, Jewel," to which I replied, "I'm so glad that I could make you proud, honey."

The nurse rushed back in the room, and before I knew it, I was once again pushing new life into the world. I was shocked at how quickly the doctor arrived and pleased that Lee did not need personal assistance from the nurse. At 8:15 in the morning, we had another baby girl with pure, perfect skin and satiny red hair, and we named her Renee.

CHAPTER

Nine

I was fond of my in-laws, and I liked Lee's friends. But I was tired of sharing my husband with them, especially now that we had two children. When Lee came home and said he could apply for a position with a food company in Ohio, I didn't hesitate to give my approval. I was more than prepared to leave college again, move eight hours away, and give up the free babysitting. After Christmas 1988, we put all our possessions in a seventeen-foot U-Haul, towing our Pontiac Grand Am, and drove it through snow and sleet to our new home on Harmony Drive, which I hoped boded well for our future.

We were buying a real home in a real neighborhood on a real cul-de-sac, and when we pulled into the driveway, the sellers were in the garage, removing the last of their possessions.

"Are you the people buying our house?" they asked us, clearly surprised.

We had two children, a mortgage, car payments, and a retirement plan, but I imagine that we looked, to them, like a couple of teenagers. Unfortunately, however, taking on new responsibilities had not cured Lee of the habits that had made me want to move in the first place. Granted, the family farm no longer claimed his attention, but drinking buddies, alcohol, and women regrettably existed all over the world.

Content at home with our two girls, Lee and I read them Dr. Suess books and The Berenstain Bears. We sang songs and sometimes danced to *Strawberry Shortcake* on the record player. Anyone passing by our open windows would likely hear giggles as we recited nursery rhymes and played tickle monster. It was a happy home with a lot of book reading, game playing, movie watching, and snack eating. I didn't care if we ever left the house, but Lee did. His social appetite needed to be fed.

"What do you think about getting a sitter for the girls and going out this weekend?" he occasionally asked.

"That'd be fine," was my usual response, which meant I didn't really want to, but I knew I needed to compromise occasionally in order to maintain a healthy marriage. We would join Lee's friends or acquaintances from work for dinner and drinks or go to someone's house. Many nights we had a nice time. Other nights I did not enjoy myself.

On one particular evening, we had been at a nightclub for several hours, and when the party began to wind down, I was ready to go to bed. We had ridden there with a few other people, and not surprisingly, I had drunk the least—which was next to nothing.

"You don't mind driving, do you?" Lee asked.

I *did* mind. I was always angry when he drank too much, and I had to be *Miss Responsibility*. "Of course, I mind," I wanted to scream. "I want to be taken care of by you. I don't want to be caring for you."

But I didn't say a word. I hoped that my silence would convey my anger, but Lee wasn't interested in how I was feeling at that time. I took the keys he handed me, and five people, all in various stages of intoxication, hopped in the back of the van. I stood outside the vehicle, hesitating but unable to muster up the courage to take a stand, particularly since I certainly didn't want to ride with someone else driving.

When I started the engine, it was clear that they were oblivious to me, whispering away to one another. Looking in the rearview mirror, I saw my husband about to take a drag on a joint.

They were using drugs! Holy crap, they were smoking pot!

Drugs were something I was totally against, and now my own husband and friends were in the process of getting high. Determined to jolt them into sobriety, I slammed my foot on the gas pedal. I wanted to wake them up. I wanted to start screaming with my righteous indignation, to remind them that we all had children at home, that drugs were not only unhealthy but illegal, and that they had the potential to ruin lives. But I said nothing and continued to drive, all the while hating them for what they were doing and what they were making me do. I wished we would get pulled over. I looked for signs of a police car, but there were none. Nothing happened; nothing changed—I just drove, and they got high.

CHAPTER

Ten

In 1977, I woke up in the middle of the night to the sound of my parents' voices. "You're so naïve, Mother," my father was saying. "You don't understand anything, and you forgive everything. You baby your grown children, and you don't get that you're not doing them any favors."

They seldom argued, and I'd never been woken up by this sort of thing before. I was only eleven, and I couldn't understand why my father was angry. I wanted to run out and defend my mother and tell him that she was the kindest woman in the world, but I didn't move. I listened for more details, but they were not forthcoming, so I curled up in a ball in my bed and prayed that God would make whatever was wrong right again until I went back to sleep.

The next morning I left my bedroom hesitantly, fully expecting my world to be changed in some drastic way.

"Would you like some eggs and bacon," my mother asked wearily, and since that tired smile wasn't unusual, I looked around for other signs that something was amiss, but everything seemed the same as usual. A radio announcer was running down the list of area birthdays, and my father was whistling as he read the newspaper in our living room. All that and the fact that bacon was sizzling on the stove made me feel so much less apprehensive that I began to wonder if I hadn't dreamt that they had had an argument.

We weren't the type of family who brought things out into the open or asked questions, so I quietly ate my breakfast and waited. I gradually detected signs that something was wrong with my brother who was eleven years older than me. He would live at home off and on, and when he was at home he engaged in what I considered to be odd behavior, which included a compulsive pacing about the house or staring out the window as though he was frightened of something. One day, when a strange car was parked in front of the house, he claimed that *they* had found him. And even though my parents reassured him that the car belonged to someone visiting the neighbors, he insisted that it was *them*, whoever *them* was.

I looked up to Jerad and wanted him to go back to being the cool brother who played the drums and was thought to be attractive by all my friends. But all he did now was sleep and pace and watch. Once he had liked to tease me and call me Wimpster, but now he ignored me. If we were in the same room, he did not see me, and if I were watching the television, he would turn it off.

I was confused, and no one was helping me to understand. My brother Joe was six years older than me and was the only other sibling still in the home, and neither he nor our parents said anything about Jerad in front of me. But because I wanted so badly for things to be the way they used to be, I baked him some of the chocolate chip slice and bake cookies that he loved, and presented him with a platter piled with them as he sat on our living room sofa. His back was straight and his hands rested on his knees. The fact that he was sitting like Abe at the Lincoln Memorial did not surprise me. It was his face that caused my steps to falter. His pale features were contorted, and tears were flowing freely down his cheeks, hitting the stubble of his unshaven skin. Some of the tears dangled from his chin until their weight became heavy enough to drop them onto his freshly laundered T-shirt.

When he took a cookie, his hand shaking, all I could say was, "If you'd like more, just let me know," before rushing back into the kitchen. I wanted him to think that I hadn't noticed anything out of the ordinary in our exchange or his behaviors, but I was fairly convinced that my brother had lost his mind and was never going to find it again.

I cried over the loss of him, and I know my mother cried too. And, as always, she prayed. Not only that, but she lit a Novena candle. She wanted to let that candle burn twenty-four hours a day, but the first night it burned, I lay in bed with a fear that was stronger than my faith. And when I heard a siren, I was convinced that burning candles through the night was not safe, so I crept down the stairway. From the bottom of the stairwell I could see the Virgin Mother glowing. I trusted her, and I believed in her, but I could not allow her shadows to bounce off the kitchen walls throughout the night. I was petrified of the curse that would come once I extinguished that flame, but I was more petrified of dying in my sleep, so I quickly put it out and turned and ran stealthily back to my room. A peaceful sleep did not come after that, but at least I was alive at dawn. I pretended to be as dumbfounded as everyone else about how that candle could have gone out, and I felt guilty because the expression on my mother's face told me that it was not a good sign.

Jerad had been married for a short while and had a baby girl, but shortly after the odd behaviors began, I didn't see his wife or child for several months. Then I would only see them when my brother was allowed to go for visits and he would take my mother and me along. We would play outside with Lisa while her mother and other grandma would watch from the window. Although Jerad was awkward around her, contenting himself with ruffling her hair and watching her play with me in the yard, he looked at her with adoring eyes, as though he was saying, "I'm not worthy of you; therefore, I can't get closer."

He eventually managed to move out of the family home and into a nearby trailer, but my mother continued to care for him. She and I would wash his dishes and clean up after him, and although he continued to be jittery and incapable of caring for himself without help, he seemed happier and sometimes would even joke with me. But my father was not as supportive. When we returned home, he would make sarcastic remarks and once actually said, "Did you smell any dope?"

From then on I was torn between feeling sorry for Jerad, because he was obviously troubled, and angry, because it all might have been caused by drug dependency. I never knew for sure, but I'm absolutely certain that it was a huge part of why I was particularly sensitive to Lee's use of drugs on that memorable night.

CHAPTER
Eleven

Thankfully, drugs were never again an issue in the marriage. Either the opportunity never presented itself, or Lee made the decision not to engage in that behavior, and the marriage endured. The moments of anger, frustration, and fighting had not yet reached the point that I had seriously considered a divorce—that is until our trip to Put-in-Bay, Ohio, during the summer of 1989. The girls were staying with their grandparents back in Iowa, so I ignored the sense of foreboding that I often felt when we were going to be in a situation that had the potential to get out of hand, and I agreed to take a trip with four other couples to a tiny two- by four-mile island on Lake Erie.

"I'm going to enjoy myself on this trip," I told Lee as we were packing our final items into our luggage. "You and I never get time away without the girls, and I'm really looking forward to it."

"I'm looking forward to it too. I'm glad you're going to be able to loosen up a little and have fun with me and our friends. Maybe we can find some time for just you and me to hang out."

"I'd really like that," I said and gave him a quick kiss on the lips and a sweet smile before we grabbed our bags and went to the car.

I probably could have counted on one hand the number of times Lee and I had engaged in activities that didn't include other people since the girls had been born, and consequently, I cherished any one-on-one time that I could get.

We arrived at our condo in the early evening. The couples who had arrived before us were already drinking and anxious for us to join them. No sooner had I sat down than someone gave me a wine cooler, which, feeling carefree, I readily accepted, eager to show my husband and our friends that I knew how to relax and have fun.

A couple of hours and a few drinks later, we decided to move on to the local pubs. Walking was not sufficient for me; I skipped. My newfound freedom from responsibility was incredibly enjoyable.

"Come on, everybody," I sang out as I bounced ahead. "Let's party. Look at all the pretty boats! Oh my goodness, this is awesome!"

Running over to Lee, I tried to jump on his back for a piggy back ride.

"I see them, Jewel," he assured me as he steadied himself and set me down firmly on the ground. I weighed 120 pounds and hardly ever drank. Everyone else had been in training for this weekend, but I was not in good drinking shape. However, I had the sense to see that I should pretend, at least, to be sober, and so I linked my arm to Lee's and walked silently beside him until we reached the Roundhouse Bar.

I imagine a regular drinker might have felt welcomed by the scent of sweat, beer, and vomit that was saturated into the wooden floors and the parachute canopy, and, had my senses not been dulled by alcohol, I might have been repulsed. As it was, however, it was not until the next day that I felt disgusted with the establishment and myself.

The bar was subdued initially due to the fact that the live band had not yet begun playing, and it was early in the evening for late night partiers. We sat around a table, ordered drinks, and told jokes as we waited for the place to liven up.

I realized that being away from the girls wasn't nearly as hard as I had thought it might be. I didn't have to drive anywhere. Lee was making us laugh, and I was enjoying myself and spending time with adults.

"Let's do a shot," I yelled. People turned to look at me, most of their faces registering shock and amusement.

"Well, okay," said one of the guys as he stood up to head toward the bar.

Lee leaned toward me and said, "Girl, you're getting crazy, and I like it."

That shot added to what I had already been drinking, plus the live band and dancing, plus my desire to let loose, equaled a free pass for me to audacious land. Most of that night is a blur, except for the part where one of the men in our group picked me up and placed me on a small, round tabletop, and I danced. I danced alone, and I danced free and easy. High above the crowd watching me, I moved my hips and pumped my arms. I felt sorry for the people that didn't get to be me, because my life was fun and exhilarating. And then, someone pulled down my elastic waistband skirt, and a bouncer made me get off the table. Within seconds, I went from emboldened to embarrassed.

The next morning, I awoke with a groan as I remembered how I had behaved the night before. Everyone else had eventually caught up with me, so no one but me was feeling as though any of us had behaved inappropriately. In fact, we lounged around most of the morning, laughing about what had happened the night before and anticipating what sort of craziness we might indulge in that night. But I made an unspoken vow to never humiliate myself to that extent again. I did not care if I drank or saw another bar.

Unfortunately, it turned out that my reckless abandon had thrilled Lee and he believed there might be a repeat performance.

But I knew better. As evening approached and drinks started flowing, I tried to make myself invisible. I did not want any attention, nor did I want to be encouraged to imbibe. Lee, however, was wearing his figurative party hat. He and two of the guys had pictures taken of their bare butts, and as I stood off to the side of the room, shaking my head, he looked at me and said the words that I had come to dread, "They're going down good tonight, sweetie."

He was referring to the drinks, and on the nights they were *going down good*, the evenings typically ended in ugly fashion. I hated to disappoint him by reverting to the uptight wife after playing the drunken dancing queen the night before, so I gave him a grin and went to talk to the girls. As the evening went on, I remained sober while the others became increasingly off-balance and silly.

Watching them from the vantage point of the couch, I tried not to judge them. *Hadn't that been me the night before?* When someone looked my way, I smiled and did a sofa dance as if I was feeling good. Actually, I was feeling relaxed, until I spied Lee going into the bathroom when, I was sure, someone had just gone in before him. Without giving myself time to think it over, I pushed my way in, and a woman I had not known before this weekend slid past me.

"Wha's up?" Lee asked me.

"What's up?" I repeatedly rather loudly, emphasizing the *up*. "What's up is that my husband was in the bathroom with another woman."

"Relax, nothin' was goin' on," he mumbled, supporting himself with his right hand outstretched to the wall above the toilet as he urinated and looked at me as though I were being ridiculous.

When he came into the bedroom later and found me looking at him with disgust, he said, "What's your problem?" and I slapped him—hard, and he reacted with a punch of his own.

It wasn't pretty. It was what I never wanted, what no one ever wants for their marriage. It wasn't a heavyweight boxer right cross punch, but it was still painful and shocking. I stared up at him, speechless. Shortly afterward, Lee passed out.

CHAPTER
Twelve

The next morning, my chin sore and my heart aching, I got up before everyone else and walked down to the bay where I sat on the dock, my legs dangling, looking out over the expanse of water and telling myself that my only option was to take Nicole and Renee and move home with my parents. *After all, I couldn't stay married, could I?* He had begun something in that bathroom with someone else, and my mind raced with the thoughts of what could have happened if I hadn't entered the room. Worse still, he had shown no remorse. Instead, he had acted as though I were in the wrong. And he had hit me.

Moving home would be difficult and humiliating. It meant moving a fair distance since they lived two states away. And besides, I didn't want to live with them, particularly since I knew they would blame me for leaving Lee. They could not provide for me and the girls. I would have to get a job, and my mother would have to care for Nicole and Renee. She had cared for many babies in her lifetime, and I didn't think she wanted to take on two more, particularly since she had spent a lifetime helping to raise, not only her own children and grandchildren, but those of her neighbors. Besides, she would be turning sixty-six in a few months and deserved a rest.

I had been fortunate enough to be a stay-at-home mom and part-time student thus far in the marriage. I wanted to be the one caring for my children, and I hated the thought of not finishing college. Logic seemed to be telling me that, in order to have what I wanted I would have to stay married. *Or would I?* I was a strong enough person to work for what I wanted without a man. But more than that, what I wanted most of all was a husband I could trust. I wanted our family to stay together, and I wanted to be happy. But that would mean I would have to forgive the events of the previous evening, and I wasn't sure I could do that.

I reminded myself that Lee and I had been married nearly four years. Wasn't that alone surprising considering how we had started. We'd probably already beaten the odds, so if we called it quits now, no one would be surprised. *But was that what I really wanted?* Just as I had felt that I needed to get married, I was also thinking I needed to stay married. Maybe we could make changes. Maybe he would be able to realize that his drinking was causing serious problems. *Hadn't I also behaved stupidly because of my drinking?* If I was willing to give it up, maybe he would too, but I doubted it.

I brought my thoughts back to the present. *Wasn't I lucky to be on this beautiful island, watching the boats in the harbor rock up and down? Wasn't I lucky to be living in a country where I had the choice to be married or not? Besides, I didn't need to decide today. Wasn't I lucky to have two beautiful children, even if they hadn't been planned?*

Taking a relieved breath, I pushed myself up from the dock, prepared to return to the man to whom I was, at present, at least, unhappily married. That thought brought a question to my mind: *Was I unhappily married in the moment or was I unhappily married in general?* It was hard to think of the good, yet I knew it was there. Lee was capable of great kindness. He was able to make me laugh, and he adored our daughters. He had good qualities, but I did not want to think of them now. I was angry, and I wanted to stay that way.

When I walked in the door of the condo, a few of the others were getting breakfast. Someone said that it had been ambitious of me to get up that early, but I just smiled as I headed toward our bedroom. Other than the bathroom floozy, no one knew there had been any problems between Lee and I, and I preferred it stayed that way. She, I knew, being a guest of one of the men, was not likely to talk about what had happened, which suited me just fine, even though I realized that it was possible that she had done nothing wrong, that it had all been Lee's fault. But, at that moment, I didn't want to think about that particular angle.

When I entered the room, I was surprised to find that Lee was awake and beginning to pack.

"Hey, Jewel," he said, "did you go for a walk already?"

Ignoring him, I began to gather my own clothes.

"You're not talking to me?" he asked, shamefaced.

"You don't want to hear what I have to say," I told him.

"Aw, jeez, here we go," he said, sighing and throwing his hands in the air.

"Here we go, what?" I demanded, meeting his eyes for the first time. "Do you even remember anything that happened last night?"

"Yeah, I got a little drunk, and things got out of hand," he admitted, "but what do you expect me to do about it now?"

It was clear from his expression that he felt no remorse, and in his face, I could no longer see the handsome, charming man with whom I had fallen in love.

"Gosh," I shot back, "I don't know, maybe you could apologize for starters."

"I'm sorry I drank too much and acted a little crazy," he said, "but you weren't exactly being an angel the night before."

I knew he would use that to shift the blame back to me. *Why had I allowed myself to get so drunk?*

"But I didn't end up in the bathroom, making out with someone, and you shouldn't have punched me," I said, loud enough that the others might have heard. But I was past caring about that.

"Oh, I barely hit you, and you slapped me first," he told me, pacing the floor and running his fingers through his hair. "And that girl and I weren't making out. We just happened to go into the bathroom at the same time."

I knew he was lying, but the marriage needed it to be the truth. *Could we tell ourselves the bathroom situation was nothing and be okay? Not yet, but maybe.*

"Look, Jewel, I'm sorry, okay? I know I messed up, but I love you. You're the one I want."

"You have a funny way of showing your love," I said more calmly.

"I know. I'll do better. I'll try harder."

He wasn't exactly begging, but I knew that he meant what he was saying. I knew he loved me, but I also knew that, with enough beer under his belt, he became someone else, someone I didn't know or want to know.

"What about the drinking?" I questioned. "This is hardly the first time you've done something stupid when you were under the influence."

"I'm not going to give up drinking," he told me defiantly. "I'm not an alcoholic. I can go weeks without having a drink. But maybe I can cut back a little during the times that I do drink. I can try. It's not like we drink that often."

His unwillingness to even consider giving up alcohol had disturbed me more than I let on. Still, although I was certain that Lee's drinking would cause us problems in the future, I had, for now, dismissed all thoughts of moving back with my parents. I needed to stay for the girls. I wanted to stay for myself.

I continued to be aloof and quiet for a few days after we returned home, and a break occurred in our sexual activity, mainly because that was the only way I knew how to punish him. But there was more to it than that. I didn't want to have sex with a man I could not completely trust or respect.

During one of Lee's remorseful moments, he had said, "You deserve better than me."

"No, I deserve you at your best," I had told him. "You have so much good in you, and I don't want to give up on that."

CHAPTER

Thirteen

Nine months. We lived in Ohio for nine months. I had gone through the application process and been accepted to school at Ohio State University, but I would never be a student there. I had gotten my associate's degree and then had taken a few classes at Western Illinois University in Macomb before we had moved to Ohio. When we moved to Pennsylvania in October of 1989, I said to Lee, "I am not leaving this state until I have my bachelor's degree."

I was accepted at Penn State University and took part-time classes at Penn State-Harrisburg while taking care of the girls and trying to start a Jazzercise business, and throughout this time period, Lee was supportive mentally, emotionally, and financially. He wanted me to be able to do what I wanted, so he worked hard and indulged me and the girls. We enjoyed our neighbors and joined a neighborhood dinner club. On football Sundays we started a fire and lay around, watching games and taking naps. We gave the girls bunnies at Easter and laughed uproariously as they chased them around the house. For our five-year anniversary, I surprised Lee by asking a neighbor to watch Nicole and Renee so that he and I could go to an inn in the Poconos where we had an incredible time, hiking, eating out, and playing in our cozy room that had a fireplace and Jacuzzi tub. Even though we had moved further from our families, we were growing closer to one another. We were enjoying marriage and our children.

On a Saturday in September of 1991, we decided to take Nicole and Renee to the Pennsylvania Renaissance Festival, which was being held within an hour-and-a-half's drive away, thinking that they would be fascinated by the medieval costumes and the jousting shows. As we drove through charming Dutch country and passed simple Amish farmhouses, the four of us were giddy with excitement. The girls were buckled in the back seat, listening to sing along songs playing from the cassette deck. When *Miss Mary Mack* came on, they sang out loudly, "Miss Mary Mack, Mack, Mack, all dressed in black, black, black, with silver buttons, buttons, buttons, all down her back, back, back!"

Nicole had Lee's blond curls and round face, while Renee, with her red, wavy hair, looked more like me. Both had a mouthful of baby teeth, and their wide smiles were bright as sunshine.

I was reveling in the moment. And then, it got even better. Lee started singing while at the same time, swerving the car from side to side to the girl's delight, "Shoo fly, don't bother me. Shoo fly, don't bother me. Cause I belong to somebody."

I was still chuckling when I noticed a horse and buggy up ahead.

"Look, girls," I said. "These people don't believe in cars and electricity. They believe God wants them to separate themselves from worldly things so they can love Him better without distractions. I think they are probably right, and we should be careful to not love things too much."

"Is it okay if I love Lola, Mommy?" Nicole asked, grabbing her water baby off the floor.

"Yes. It's okay to love Lola," I responded, "but make sure you always love your sister, your mom and dad, and God the most, okay?"

Nicole nodded her head and then gave her water baby a squeeze. Renee started a list, "I love God and Jesus and Mommy and Daddy and Nicole and Grandma and Grandpa and my cousins and…"

Nicole interrupted, "We get it, Renee, jeez."

"How about another song?" questioned Lee in an attempt to avoid a backseat squabble. He pushed the button to restart the tape, and we all sang, "The wheels on the bus go round and round, round and round, round and round."

I can still remember how happy we were.

When we arrived at the sixteenth century festival and walked through the gates, we were deluged with sights and sounds. Magnificently costumed characters were everywhere, and the sound of recorders and harps, together with the smell of beer and roasting turkey legs, made this a wonderful feast for the senses until, that is, I became aware that my husband would be feasting his eyes upon a good deal of cleavage. Everywhere I turned, boobs were bursting out of too tight Gothic gowns. It was a virtual cleavage carnival, and while I was not surprised, I did not want Lee to embarrass us.

"This would be a good time to work on the art of glancing, instead of gawking," I suggested.

"What do you mean?" he asked as he began imitating a cartoon character whose eyeballs bounce in and out of his head at the sight of a pretty woman.

"You're pathetic," I replied. "Come on, girls. Let's find Daddy a jousting show to watch."

Although there was no jousting in sight, there were blacksmiths plying their trade, and weaving demonstrations, as well as quaint booths where jewelry, pottery, and swords were on sale. Ahead of us, I noticed the strength-testing game. The young man dressed as a knight, standing next to the attraction, was holding the mallet, calling out, "Step right up, ladies and gentleman, and test your strength."

"You should try that out, honey," I told Lee. "Show me what a big, strong man you are. Here, let me get the camera."

"I'm not sure I need to do that," he said. "You already know how strong I am, baby."

I figured he wouldn't want to do it, not because he was concerned about his ability to do well, as a husky farm boy, he had swung more than his share of mallets when splitting wood, but because, in Lee's mind, it would have been a waste of a few dollars. He had been tight with money throughout the marriage, and the fact that he had paid the admission fee without grumbling or asking for a discount from the ticket agent had already been a surprise, and I didn't want to push the matter. We stood and watched someone else try his luck and laughed when the puck drained of energy only halfway to the bell. I looked down to see if the girls were enjoying themselves, but only Nicole was standing there.

"Where's Renee?" I demanded, instantly on high alert.

"I thought she was right here," Lee said.

Grabbing Nicole's hand, I went off in one direction and Lee in another. But there was no sign of her. I was in my worst nightmare. *Oh, dear God, let Renee be okay. Please let her be okay. Please, God. Please, God.* I repeated over and over again. *Please, God, let her be safe. Please don't allow someone to have taken her. Please, please, please.*

"We need to find someone who works here to help us," Lee said grimly.

I spotted a man not far away in a vest with a Renaissance Festival patch on his breast and noticed that he was wearing a walkie-talkie.

"Our daughter is missing," I cried, running over to him. "Can you help us, please? Her name is Renee, and she has red hair and blue eyes and is wearing a flowered top with pink shorts and tennis shoes."

He pushed the button on the two-way radio and conveyed the description to whoever was listening. He concluded by saying, "Have someone watching all the gates."

Envisioning some creep carrying my beautiful baby girl out to his car and doing unspeakable things to her, I wanted to break down, but I couldn't. Nicole was watching my every move, and I knew she was frightened. *Oh, God,* I started again, *Please let her be okay. Please let them find her. Please let them find her.*

Lee's eyes met mine. "She'll be okay," he said. "She has to be okay. She's my little Lou Lou."

"Oh, God, I hope she's all right," I responded.

The few minutes that passed seemed like an eternity before the man in the vest received word that she had been found and that she had been taken to the children's play area.

As soon as we got there and spotted her, talking to one of the female employees, I rushed to take her in my arms, and both of us started crying.

"Mommy," she said. "I was scared for you."

"I was scared for you too, sweetie," I told her. "Mommy's so glad you are okay, and I'm so sorry we lost you. I'm so sorry."

Lee and Nicole joined in our hug, and I noticed Lee's eyes were wet as well.

"She was a smart girl," said one of the employees. "She went straight to one of the vendors and asked for help."

"She's my smart, amazing Lou Lou," said Lee as he picked her up and bounced her around.

Hugging her daddy tightly around the neck, she began to giggle.

"Can we go home?" I asked him. "I've had my fill of the fair."

"You girls okay with that?" he asked Nicole and Renee.

"Yeah, but can we get some ice cream?" asked Nicole.

"Ice cream sounds like a great idea," Lee told her. "How about we stop at a Dairy Queen on the way home?"

Suddenly, everything was back to normal. But I knew I would never forget the sheer terror of nearly having lost one of my little girls. I praised God silently, as Lee swung Renee up onto his shoulders. With Nicole's hand in mine, I wrapped my other arm around Lee's waist, and we were a family again.

Once we were safely back in the car, Lee reached over and squeezed my hand.

"For a moment I thought we had lost her forever," he said in a low voice as the girls engaged in a conversation about some game they intended to play when they got home. "I was so scared."

"Me too," I told him. "I was praying so hard. Weren't you?"

"Actually, I was too busy looking for her to pray," he told me, starting the car.

"You mean you didn't pray at all?" I asked.

How could that be? How could he not have prayed? We took the girls to church nearly every Sunday and said the *Our Father* with them every night. Faith was woven into my very being, and yet it hadn't even occurred to him to pray. *If faith doesn't guide him,* I thought, *what does?*

"You might want to say a prayer of thanksgiving," I suggested.

"Yeah," he said. "I should."

CHAPTER

Fourteen

In late February of 1992, Lee came home from work and shared the news that he was being transferred to Missouri, and he would start his new job in two weeks. We'd almost made it until I had my degree. I was in my final semester of college and would finish student teaching in the middle of May. I was pregnant again and due at the end of September. This time it had been planned, and we were thrilled.

We decided that Lee would take Renee with him back to the Midwest, and she could stay with his mother during the week, and he would be with her during the weekend while I would keep Nicole with me so she could finish kindergarten. It wasn't ideal, but it would only be for a couple of months, and it would allow me to move to Missouri with a bachelor's degree in English Education.

Although we had made friends and enjoyed Pennsylvania, we were looking forward to being closer to home and living in the state where we met. I realized right away that the couple of months of separation were going to be difficult, even though Lee and Renee were planning to make a trip back to Pennsylvania. I missed them. I didn't want to be apart from my baby girl or my husband. One week later while I was talking to Lee on the telephone, I broke down.

"I can't wait a month to see her," I told him, sobbing.

His first response was to tell me to stop being a baby, but then, after I hung up on him, he called back and said he was sorry and asked me what I needed him to do.

I didn't know what I needed. I just knew I missed them. We didn't have enough money for them to fly out more than once, so I would have to figure out how to deal with it. I suppose all I wanted was my husband to be understanding about my sadness. I wanted to feel as if he missed me too and was desperate to see me.

I made it through the next few weeks, busying myself with taking care of Nicole and concentrating on school. In early April, she and I went to the Harrisburg International Airport to pick up Lee and Renee. I was so excited to see my baby girl and husband again. Airport security was more relaxed in the early nineties, and we were able to wait right outside of the gate. We saw their plane pull up, and I watched with anticipation as people began filing out. From where I stood, I could see down the narrow walkway, and suddenly, there they were, Renee carrying a mini backpack and Lee following close behind. I ran down to meet them with Nicole trailing behind, and I fell to my knees to take my baby in an embrace.

"Lou Lou, Mommy missed you so much," I cried, tears running down my cheeks, only to feel her stiffen in my arms.

"Julie," I heard Lee say. "You're embarrassing her. Maybe we should get out of everyone's way."

Picking Renee up, I led the way back into the terminal, where we all shared a family hug.

When the time came for them to fly back to Kansas City, it was not as difficult as the first time. I knew when we saw one another again, we would be starting life together in another state, and we had gotten good at that.

CHAPTER

Fifteen

The week before Penn State's commencement ceremony, we moved into our ranch style house in the Show Me State. A change from the two split-level homes we had previously lived in, it sat on top of a hill on three acres at the edge of town. Behind us was a neighborhood and in front of us, at the bottom of our winding gravel driveway, a two-lane highway separated us from a field, in which cows grazed. This was our compromise, the best of both worlds.

I woke up on the Saturday morning of my graduation day saddened that I was unable to walk across the stage and get my diploma. It had taken me a total of eight years of taking classes in five states, and six schools, counting the college courses I had taken in high school, and the abortive enrollment at Ohio State, to earn this four-year degree, and I was understandably proud of the fact that I had done this while raising two amazing little girls and building a marriage. It was only natural that I would have liked my family to see me in cap and gown. Apparently aware that I was a bit gloomy, Lee suggested that we mark the day by doing something special.

"We can go out for lunch and walk around the mall," he said. "Maybe we'll buy you a graduation present."

His parents, who had come to help us move and were going to be staying with us for a few days, were more than willing to care for the girls. So Lee and I left a little before noon and shared a lunch at The Ground Round and then window shopped at the mall, where he insisted on buying me a dishtowel. My confusion only lasted until we got to the car.

"Hold it over your face," he said. "I'm taking you somewhere special, and I don't want you to know where we're going, so please hold that over your face, and don't peek."

"Where are you taking me, sweetie?" I asked without expecting an answer. "You're not taking me out in the middle of nowhere to have sex with me are you?"

"Well, that wasn't what I had planned, but if that's what your little heart desires, I guess I could change my plans," he said, putting the key in the ignition.

"Let's stick with the original plan," I said, giggling as he placed the towel over my face. "I promise not to peek."

As we drove, my gloom gave way to giddiness as I tried to track the turns we were making in an attempt to figure out where he might be taking me, but it seemed we were going in circles. I truly had no idea what his surprise could be, so I relaxed and entertained myself by wondering what other drivers would think if they saw me.

"Are we about there?" I asked after about ten minutes.

"Not much further," he said, and I could tell from the lilt in his voice that he was as excited as I was.

When we stopped, he secured the dishtowel around my head and helped me out of the car. There were steps, and I heard a door open. And then, suddenly the strains of *Pomp and Circumstance* filled the air. Then, when Lee removed my blindfold, I found that we were in our own living room and that it was filled with my loved ones: my parents, my siblings, and friends.

Lee and I looked at one another, both our eyes filled with tears. "Congratulations, honey," he said, and kissed me.

The guests then surrounded us, and I hugged them one by one. Most had driven at least four hours to come and celebrate with me. One of my sister's husbands showed me the invitation that Lee had had printed, and even though it was far from professionally done and featured a number of misspellings, I thought it was magnificent. Until then, I had not believed it was possible for my husband to keep a secret, let alone be so thoughtful.

I spent the rest of the day visiting, opening gifts, eating cheeseburgers that Lee grilled, and filling up on a chocolate chip cookie cake that read "Congratulations Penn State Graduate." Lee had thought of everything, and that night I thanked him.

CHAPTER

Sixteen

During my last semester at Penn State, I had written a paper for English Composition entitled *Knock on Wood*, in which I expostulated on the essential perfection of my marriage. Lee and I weren't wealthy or famous, but we had a warm home, two beautiful children, and our health. We had overcome the unpromising conditions of the way we had begun and made a success of our lives. A few years later, I would look back on that writing assignment with embarrassment, knowing that my life had been flawed in ways that I had never imagined.

If anything, the move to Missouri increased my false sense of well-being. We were closer to our families, but not too close. We made fantastic friends right away. Lee worked within five minutes of our home, and our girls adjusted quickly to their new environment. We also began attending a wonderful church. I thought we had perfected perfection.

One Sunday, a couple of months after the move from Pennsylvania, I was looking over the church bulletin on the way home from mass.

"What would you think about having a nun live with us?" I asked Lee as he drove down the highway toward our house.

"A nun!" he exclaimed, almost driving off the road. "What the hell! Don't they have places for them to live?"

"Well, I'm sure they do, but this one wants to go to school at the local college for a semester, and she needs somewhere to stay. Our basement has an empty bedroom, and it's practically its own apartment down there."

"Why's a nun going to school anyway?" he demanded. "Don't they just pray all time? And I thought they lived in convents."

"I don't know the specifics of the situation," I said, annoyed. "All I know is that the bulletin is asking for someone to provide housing for a nun for a few months, and we have the space."

"Well, would she pay rent?"

"I don't know, Lee," I said patiently. "I just thought we could do it out of the goodness of our hearts as a way of giving back, since we are so blessed."

"You're right. It would be a nice thing," he conceded, "but I don't know about having somebody else in our house, especially a nun. We got a good thing going now with you, me, and the girls, and we're going to be pretty busy with the baby when it comes in a few months."

"That's true," I said, "but if the baby comes quickly or during the night, we'd have someone at the house to stay with the girls."

I didn't want to drop the subject. I'm not sure if I really wanted to have a nun stay with us or if I wanted to test Lee's love for me and see if I could get my way. Certainly, I was aware that some people would consider this an unusual, if not extreme request.

"I don't know, Jewel," he said, flipping on the turn signal, with a little more force than necessary, as we slowed to exit the highway. "People might think I've strayed, and you had to bring a nun into our home to straighten me out."

"What do we care what people think," I said, going along with the joke. "Now that you mention it, maybe she will help me keep you in line."

Sister Tiahn from Vietnam moved in with us a few weeks later. Other than the one morning Lee walked out in his underwear as she was leaving for school, her time with us was unremarkable. However, the fact that Lee had been gracious enough to agree to her stay added, unfortunately, to my sense of security in the marriage. I took it as a sign that the marriage was healthy, and Lee and I were on the right path.

CHAPTER

Seventeen

One afternoon in late September we received a phone call from Lee's brother, informing us that his wife had just given birth to a son. Lee's parents had their first grandson, and my father-in-law, his first namesake. We, of course, were happy for them, but we were also jealous. We wanted a son. *How much longer would we have to wait and wonder about our own child?*

As it turned out, we didn't have to wait long. Later that same night, Lee left me, snuggled up on the couch, reading a book to Renee, to watch Monday Night Football at a local sports bar. At about the time the cow jumped over the moon, I felt something I'd never felt before—a small burst of warm liquid between my legs. I didn't want to startle Renee, so I said, "Mommy's going potty. I'll be right back."

Poor little Renee had already been frightened once earlier in the day when I slept past the time to pick her up from preschool. After dropping her off, I had gone back home and sat down with a magazine. Feeling tired, I decided to rest my eyes for a minute, only to be awakened by the phone over two and a half hours later. It was her preschool teacher, asking if someone was on the way to pick her up.

Wondering why on earth I had napped for more than my usual half hour, I raced to the school to find Renee standing on the curb with her teacher, looking relieved, disappointed, and embarrassed. As she hurried to the car and got in without a word, I knew that I was once again the mother who had lost her at the Renaissance Festival.

"I'm so sorry, hon," I told her. "Mommy fell asleep, but I'll never do that again."

Now, although I didn't want to frighten her twice in one day, I was pretty sure that my water had broken—which did, indeed turn out to be the case.

But when I called the bar to tell Lee to come home, the woman who answered informed me that they weren't supposed to page people during Monday Night Football.

Frustrated, I called my friend, Shelly, asked Sister Tiahn to watch the girls, and gathered my things together, so we could stop at the bar and transfer me to Lee's Jeep Wrangler.

"He says he'll be out at halftime," Shelly told me, grinning when she came out. "But he was just joking. I know how badly he wants this baby."

All our friends knew how important it was for Lee to have a son and often regaled one another by telling how he had read *How to Determine the Sex of Your Baby* from cover-to-cover before I conceived. During the ultrasound, though, we hadn't wanted to find out for sure just yet.

We arrived at the hospital at around nine, and a nurse wheeled me to the birthing suite while Lee ran ahead to get the game on the television. Once I was settled, the contractions that had been mild became intense enough so that it was difficult for me to focus on the game, and I grabbed his hand and began to squeeze it. He squeezed back without taking his eyes off the TV. It was clear to me what was taking precedent at that particular moment.

The game finally ended with the Kansas City Chiefs beating the Oakland Raiders twenty-seven to seven, which Lee took as a good omen, despite the fact that, as the contractions worsened, I was no longer a pleasant companion. I didn't turn into a she-devil as I had when I was in labor with Nicole, but I became focused and uncommunicative. The nurse told me I was doing a good job of breathing through the contractions, and I was dilating at a rapid pace. *Thank goodness.*

The doctor came in sometime before midnight, outfitted with his mask and blue scrubs, and settled down to probe and cut. As for Lee, now a master hand at this, he observed everything with admirable calm. When the command came to push, I wasted no time in complying. I could feel the baby slipping from me.

"What a pretty face," commented the observing nurse.

"And red hair," added the doctor.

I practically sat up straight. "Are you telling me that's it's a girl?" I demanded.

"We don't know that yet," said the nurse. "We need a few more pushes."

I relaxed back until the next contraction urged me to press forward again and again until I heard the most wonderful words in the world.

"It's a boy!"

Lee had tears in his eyes. And so did I.

It was one minute after midnight, and we had our son, Tyler.

CHAPTER
Eighteen

Tyler was the first baby we had planned, and we wanted the world to know that we had a son. We wanted to shout it from the rooftops. On the day that we brought him home, I was sitting on the couch, nursing him when Lee said, "The girls and I are going to do something, but I'm not going to tell you what it is, because you might try to stop us."

"So why are you even telling me about it?" I asked him, distractedly.

"Cause we're going outside for a while, and we might be making some noises, and I don't want you to worry," he explained.

If it had not been for the fact that I was so absorbed in the sheer wonder of holding this baby in my arms, I might have asked more questions, but I scarcely paid any attention to what was going on until I heard footsteps on the roof.

At first what I was hearing didn't really penetrate because I was so absorbed in looking at Tyler, who had now fallen asleep, trying to memorize how he looked, perfect and precious, and everything we had wanted. I already knew, in the years ahead, I would find it hard to be angry with him for even the worst offense. Lee didn't want more children, and I didn't want another badly enough to argue with him, so Tyler would be our only boy and last child. I would smother him with love every day.

As I gazed at his round, pink face, light eyelashes and brows, and red, silk hair, I prayed silently: *Dear Lord, thank You for this amazing son. Thank You for the blessings You continue to bestow upon my life. Please watch over him and our family, and keep us happy, healthy and safe.*

At that moment, I was jolted back into reality when I became more aware of the thumping on our ranch house roof.

Please, Lord, don't let Lee have taken the girls up on the roof, I went on, wondering what on earth he could be doing. *How like Lee,* I thought irritably. Here I had been sitting quietly with the baby, when he had apparently decided to get up to something that would make me worry. *Couldn't he just leave well enough alone?*

When the thumping continued, I finally became so curious, not to mention concerned, that I put Tyler in his bassinette, threw on a jacket, and was just starting out the door when Lee and the girls, both of them giggling, came into the kitchen from the garage.

"We have a surprise, Momma," Renee said. "Want to see?"

"Yes, I do," I replied. "I've been hearing someone on the roof, and I was wondering what you have been up to. I was praying that you weren't up there, baby girl."

"No, we didn't get on the roof, but we were Daddy's helpers," Nicole told me, taking my hand. "Come and see what we did."

"Cover your eyes first," Lee told me.

They led me into the front yard and through the grass toward the road.

"Okay, Momma, turn around, and you can look," Nicole said to me as she let go of my hand.

Uncovering my eyes, I turned and looked at the house. There on the roof, written in large, block, pastel-colored letters with chalk, it read, "It's a boy."

"Isn't it great, Momma?" Renee asked me, beaming.

"Yes, love, it's pretty impressive," I agreed. "Everyone driving on the highway or flying overhead is going to know we have a new baby boy."

I stared with awe at the blue, green, and pink letters spread across the top of our house. Lee had said he didn't want to tell me what he was doing because I might try to stop him.

"Is it okay that I did this?" Lee asked, putting one arm around me.

"Of course," I replied, making a mental note to be more tolerant and kind. "It's a great way to let the world know how excited we are."

As the three of us went back into the house and surrounded the bassinet for one more look at the little boy who would make our family complete, I thought that I had never been so happy.

CHAPTER

Nineteen

I had the opportunity to return the surprise and demonstrate my love for my husband when his thirtieth birthday came around in the spring of 1993. He had been working a good deal of overtime, and even though the big day fell on a weekend, he had to work the second shift until three in the morning. We didn't typically make a big deal out of one another's birthdays, but I wanted to do something nice to let him know I appreciated how hard he had been working.

And so, I set the alarm for two forty-five, and when it went off, brushed my teeth, put on makeup, and fixed my hair loose and curly in a ponytail before going to the kitchen to take out the German chocolate cake that I had baked earlier in the evening. I stuck candles in it, enough to light it up, but not so many that I couldn't get them all lit between the time I heard the garage door go up and the time he walked in the door.

Finally, with just a few minutes to spare, I threw off my pajamas, slipped into my sexiest high-heeled shoes, put on Lee's nicest tie, and turned off all the lights except for one lamp in the corner of our dining area.

At exactly seven minutes past three, I heard the rumble of the garage door and knew it was time for the show to begin. When the door opened, I was seductively posed in the kitchen chair with my ankles crossed and my fancy feet on the edge of the table.

It took Lee, stunned into silence, a few minutes to register what he was seeing. I giggled to myself as I realized my face was the last thing he was taking in.

"How was your day, dear?" I asked, copying Julia Robert's line and look from *Pretty Woman*.

"Oh my," he said. "I bet you're freezing your ass off."

I wished he had stayed silent.

"That's not exactly the response I was looking for," I said.

"Oh, yeah, sorry," he said, wide-eyed. "This is awesome. I can't believe it. My brother's not going to believe it either. Can I take a picture?"

So this was all the response I was going to get. He wanted to take my picture so he could show it to his brother and probably to *the boys*, as well.

"I'm trying to do something romantic," I told him. "Couldn't you at least try to play along with that?"

"Jewel, I'm sorry…" he said again. "I guess I'm just in shock. I don't know what to say. Let me get a closer look at you. Nice tie!"

"Who looks better, me or Vivian?" I questioned.

"Vivian?" he asked, but he quickly remembered that was Julia Roberts's character name and added, "oh, you definitely look better than Vivian."

"Yeah, right," I responded with disbelief in my voice. I had put him in a no win situation.

"No, seriously, Julia Roberts ain't got nothing on you, baby. You look hot!"

"Whatever," I said. "You're just hoping to get lucky."

"Well, hell yeah, I'm hoping to get lucky. You look good, sweetie." He could have left it at that, but he didn't. "And what are we going to do with this cake?" he asked suggestively.

"Hmm, well, I know it's your birthday and all, but I think the only thing we're going to be doing with that cake is eating it."

"That's exactly what I want to do with it, but I don't want to eat it off a plate," he said, assuming an excellent approximation of a leer.

"So much for romance," I muttered. "Let's go to bed. You were right. I'm freezing."

He hugged my nude body to him, and I snuggled in.

"Thank you," he whispered in my ear. "You're the greatest."

After making love, I lay, thinking about our relationship. It certainly wasn't perfect, but we did have fun together. He wasn't exactly *Mr. Suave*, but he made me laugh.

Please be with us and our children, Lord, I prayed. *Please continue to be with us*. And then, I slept the peaceful slumber of a woman satisfied with her life, if only for a short while longer.

CHAPTER
Twenty

One of the bonuses of our relationship was the fact that we supported one another. During the first years of our marriage, when I wanted to earn money from home by making ceramic owls and painting them, he supported me, although I never completed a single one. When it took four colleges across five states for me to complete my undergraduate degree, he had been encouraging and accommodating. And when we lived in Pennsylvania, and I had wanted to start a Jazzercise franchise, he was behind me, even though it never quite took off.

In return, I had supported his career as it had taken us from Iowa to Ohio to Pennsylvania to Missouri. And when he came home from work one afternoon in the summer of 1994, and said, "They want me to work out of California for a few months," I tried to ignore the unrest that I felt, and I supported him. Lee was the type of person who embraced change and abhorred becoming stagnant, especially with regards to his work. He also loved being put in charge of projects and enjoyed traveling, so I knew this opportunity would be thrilling for him, if not for me, particularly when I soon found out that he had considerably minimized the length of time this project was supposed to take.

Soon after Lee had shared his news with me about his upcoming work travel plans, a coworker of his hosted a murder mystery dinner party, at which I was asked to appear as a hooker and Lee a hiker. When we arrived at the party, me scantily clad and him looking like he should yodel, we found ourselves in the company of a police officer, a movie star, a millionaire, a cabana boy, and a half dozen other potential killers. I was only mildly uncomfortable in my classless costume and was having an enjoyable evening until the attractive actress asked how I felt about Lee spending the next six months working in California.

The words *six months*, bounced from one ear to another like a ping pong ball. I'm sure the woman only asked out of interest, but I despised her for it, as well as everyone who was listening. They were all from his world: the corporate world, a world in which bottom lines were all important, and I was an outsider. All of them knew what was really going on, and I had been provided with half-truths. Seeing that Lee was looking askance at me, I assumed the smile of the seasoned prostitute and said, "I just do what my john tells me to do. It'll be fine," at which everyone chuckled and the evening went on.

I managed to keep an air of calm about me throughout the night as we figured out we weren't murderers, but I would have liked to strangle my husband. As soon as we got in the car to go home, I said, "Six months?"

"I know I didn't say six," he protested. "I said 'A few,' which is close. Besides, we're not really sure how long it is going to take."

"You and I both know that *a few* typically means three," I said. "Not half a year. And I absolutely hate it when other people, especially attractive women, have information about you that I don't. It was almost like she knew I didn't know it was going to be that long and was rubbing it in my face."

"She wasn't trying to rub it in your face. She was just asking a question and getting you involved in the conversation."

"Well, isn't she just super! That was so kind of her to bring up a sensitive topic in front of everyone and put me on the spot like that! My husband is leaving me to be a single mother for six months, and she wants to know how I feel about it. You're right; she's so kind!"

"I didn't say she was kind," he told me nervously, rubbing the steering wheel as though it were a stress ball. "I just said she was trying to involve you. Look, I know you're upset about me working in California for six months, but bottom line, there's nothing I can do about it, unless you want me to quit my job."

"So if you don't take on this project, you're going to get fired? Really?"

"I don't know if I would get fired," he said, "but I want to do this. I think it could be fun for me and us. I'll fly back every other weekend, and you can fly out to see me a couple of times. We can also have a family vacation out there, and it will practically be paid for by the company, because they'll pay for your flights, and I'll have a place for us to stay. Can't we look at this like an adventure?"

I silently pondered that question. I was often encouraging others to see challenges in a positive light. I would sometimes tell Nicole and Renee when they were grouchy or upset about a trivial matter, "Happiness is a choice." He was going, and I had to choose how I was going to deal with it. *Taking a couple of trips to sunny California might not be horrendous*, I told myself, and it wasn't like I had to juggle a full-time job while being a single mom. I was working only a few hours a week as a fitness instructor at the YMCA, and I wouldn't really be a single parent. Lee would be making trips back for the weekends, and we would talk on the phone. I would still have his support. And, I suppose I needed to give him mine without conditions.

"It'll be fine," I said, not willing to concede anything more than that. "I'm sure it'll be fine."

"You hate *fine*," he commented, and he was right. Ever since I was a teenager and my mother would tell me I looked fine when I wanted to look great, I had hated that word.

"It'll have to do for now," I said, "'cause I'm still mad at you for lying to me."

"I'm sorry for that, but I didn't really lie. I just didn't tell the whole truth, because I didn't want to upset you."

I let out a sigh. "Can you just say I'm sorry without the *buts*, please, because that causes me to get upset all over again."

"I'm sorry," he said, and I believed that he meant it. The apologies that came after his transgressions were usually sincere, but if I'd had a sorry bucket, it would have been about half full, and in a few years the sorrys would be flowing over the sides.

CHAPTER
Twenty-One

The six months turned out to be eight during which time we took a family vacation to Disneyland and I visited Lee once by myself. We had been able to see one another about every two or three weeks, but in his absence, I had honed my skills as a single mom. Initially, adjusting to having him home again was difficult. The kids and I had a routine, and I felt like he sometimes got in our way. I wasn't disappointed when he had to make regular bimonthly trips to check on the project's progress.

He and I had grown distant, not only from one another, but from our friends, so when Shelly and her husband, John, invited us to go out with them on a Friday night, we considered it an opportunity to reconnect with them and each other. They had a good relationship, and that encouraged us to work on our own. We made plans to meet at Legends Sports Bar for dinner. I was looking forward to it, and it was going well until halfway into the meal when Lee, who was drinking bourbon and Pepsi, said, "They're going down good tonight, sweetie."

He said it as if it would be thrilling news, but as far as I was concerned, it wasn't even close. Whenever he said that, I was no longer able to relax and enjoy myself. I became a dual personality:

a frightened child, terrified of what he was going to do once he was drunk, and a responsible caretaker, who had to keep him from making the horrible decisions he always made when he was in that condition. Over the years, I've wondered whether he used my sanctimonious responses to excuse whatever bad behavior he decided to indulge in. As long as he could characterize me as a nag, anything that he did was justified.

Our friends knew nothing of the quiet storm that had begun to develop between Lee and me, not only on this night but over the last several months. I'm not even sure Lee was aware of it. We continued with the lighthearted conversation, and when the drinks didn't come fast enough, Lee headed to the bar. My eyes followed him, knowing with some certainty that he would find an attractive female to chat with while waiting for his drink. There were two of them sitting together, long hair, cute, and dying for someone like my husband to take interest in them. When he smiled at them and said something that made them laugh, my stomach churned.

Our friends were, I realized, watching me warily.

"We told the sitter we were having dinner and would be home by ten," Shelly said. "We're probably going to have to go in a few minutes."

"Yeah, that's fine," I said as Lee came back. "We're probably going to have to get going, too."

"I just got myself a fresh drink," Lee complained, raising his glass in the air so suddenly that the liquor nearly sloshed over the edge. "We can't go yet."

After our friends left, Lee and I sat there, me feeling tense, him appearing quite relaxed. Since he wasn't saying a word, I was sure he was aware of my displeasure and the disturbance to the atmosphere between us, and I was certain that he didn't care. From my seat at a right angle to him, I could see his gaze alternate between looking at the basketball game on the big screen television and checking out his new friends at the bar. After he had taken a few swigs of his drink and continued with his eye dance, my tolerance gauge hit empty.

"Would you like me to ask them to join us?" I asked him.

"What are you talking about?"

"Or maybe I could ask them to come over and do a slow spin, so you could check them out from every angle?"

"What's your problem?" he asked.

"My problem is you've had too much to drink, I'm ready to go, and I'm tired of watching my husband check out the tramps at the bar."

They could have been perfectly nice people and probably were, but the fact that they had my husband's attention made them trash in my book.

"You're ready to go, huh? Fine," he said as he threw back the last third of his drink, grabbed his jacket off the back of the chair, and headed toward the door.

We'd already paid for our meal, so I dug through my purse for some tip money, threw it on the table, and hurried outside.

"I'm not letting you drive in that condition," I told him. "Give me the keys."

"I'm fine," he replied angrily, sliding into the driver's seat. "Get in!"

I opened the door on the passenger's side, leaned in, and said, "I just don't feel comfortable—"

That was when he stepped on the gas, hurling me inside. I pulled my legs in right before the door slammed shut.

"You're an idiot!" I cried. "What are you trying to do? You could have killed me!"

Shaking with anger, I stared wide-eyed at the stranger beside me.

"Settle down," he told me, slurring his words. "I didn't hurt you."

That was when I slapped him, and the car swerved.

"Don't ever do that again!" he shouted, squeezing my hand.

I didn't hit him again, but I wanted to, over and over until his drinking didn't hurt me anymore.

"I can't believe what a jerk you are," I told him. "I hate being married to you!"

If I couldn't hurt him physically, I would try to hurt him emotionally. It didn't work.

"You've got it so good with me," he said. "I go to work all day, every day, and you get to stay home and play with the kids. You couldn't survive without me."

"Is that right?" I retorted. "Well, I certainly could find somebody better than you. You've gained thirty pounds since we got married, you travel more than half the time, and when you are here, you treat me like crap."

None of my responses were those of an educated, Christian woman, but since I was angry, because I wanted a godly husband, I figured God would forgive me. Lee and I were still fighting when we reached our home.

Lee didn't pull into the garage, but stopped outside of it, which meant he intended to leave again once I got out of the car. When he put the car in park, I reached over and turned the key off, pulled it from the ignition, and ran into the house. He came in after me but didn't hurry.

"Give me the keys to the car," he said firmly.

I relieved the babysitter, who could walk across the yard to her house, and then, still clutching the keys, I told him that he had no business driving in his condition and went into the bedroom. But before I could slam the door, he grabbed my hand.

He swore. "Give me the keys."

I didn't think he would hurt me, but I wasn't sure, so I gave them to him, and he left the house.

When I heard him come in at a little after one in the morning and go straight to the extra bedroom, I knew better than to expect an apology or decent conversation. I was fairly sure that the apology would come after he had slept it off, but I wasn't at all certain that I would accept it. We had fought about the drinking and flirting for ten years, and I felt like it would never change. Just as I had the morning after our big fight in Ohio, I lay in bed in Missouri, pondering my few options. This time I had three children to consider instead of two, and my faith had grown to the point that I could hear God say to me more clearly than before, "This is the man you chose to marry. You need to continue making the marriage work."

CHAPTER
Twenty-Two

The apology didn't come in the morning. We side-stepped one another for the better part of the day, and I made my anger known through my one word responses to his lame questions:

"Do you want to order pizza for lunch?"

"Whatever."

"Do you know where my shorts that I like to work out in are?"

"No."

"Can we just forget about what happened last night?"

"Screw you." Of course, I had to pull out my favorite response at some point.

Later that night I was standing in the bathroom in my pajamas, taking off my mascara with Vaseline when Lee came in.

"I'm sorry about what happened," he said as, continuing my nightly routine, I ignored him. "That wasn't the way I wanted the night to go."

"It wasn't?" I retorted, turning to look him in the eyes. "You mean to tell me you didn't intentionally get drunk, flirt with other women, drag me from a moving vehicle, and then grab me when I didn't want to give you the keys to drive drunk? And here I thought you planned all that because you thought it would be fun."

"Why do you always have to be so sarcastic?" he asked me, sighing. "I was looking forward to spending some time together last night and things got a little out of hand, and I'm sorry."

"You're sorry? Things got a *little* out of hand?" I said angrily. "Do you have any idea how many times you have said that to me? I'll be as sarcastic as I damn well please, because I'm sick and tired of your *sorrys* and *out of hands*."

"I know you are," he said wearily. "I'm sick of saying them. I want to figure out a way to make things different for us. I don't want this to keep happening."

"Well, what's your grand idea?" I demanded. "Do you think you're going to give up drinking? Because I can tell you right now that will never happen."

"I don't know, Jewel," he said, raking his fingers through his hair. "But I realize that I need to change things. I'm really sorry about last night. I'm such an idiot, and I know it, but I do love you and the kids."

I believed him, but I didn't have much hope for change. "I'm going to bed," I said. "I'm fresh out of ideas, not to mention forgiveness."

The next morning, when I was getting the kids ready for church, Lee appeared, wearing a royal blue dress shirt, nicely pressed black slacks, and dress shoes.

"Daddy, you look so handsome," Renee told him.

"Thanks, baby," he said, posing like a runway model. "I'm dressing up for God today."

"Yeah, you look really nice, Daddy," added Nicole.

I, of course, didn't say a word. He did look exceptionally nice, because he had also put gel in his hair and was freshly shaven, but I certainly wasn't going to feed his ego by giving him an admiring once-over. I put Tyler's little arms in the sleeves of his jacket and tried to ignore the fact that the girls were so excited about the appearance of a man who should have been dressing up every Sunday.

"Don't you think Daddy looks handsome, Mommy?" Nicole asked, to my chagrin. The children were extremely adept at knowing when I was annoyed with Lee, and they liked to help patch up our differences by making us talk to each other.

"Yes," I said. "He looks fine, but all this *oohing* and *ahhing* over him is going to make us late, so can everyone please go get in the car?"

As it often happens, the lesson that day matched our situation.

"God asks us to turn away from sin and turn to him," Father Murphy declared from the pulpit. "Jesus answered the people, 'It is not the healthy who need a physician, but those who are sick. I have not come to call the righteous, but sinners to repentance.'"

I felt smug. But then it occurred to me that my own self-righteousness made me a sinner. Not, perhaps, like Lee, but a sinner all the same. And yet, even if my anger was a sin, it didn't change the fact that it was Lee's fault that I was angry in the first place. *In fact, if it weren't for Lee, I would probably be perfect.* The idea amused me so much that I almost laughed aloud. And, perhaps, God chuckled too.

The sermon must have also held some sort of revelation for Lee, because, in the car, on the way home, he announced that he was going to become a Catholic, proving once again that whatever else he was, he was a man who was full of surprises.

CHAPTER

Twenty-Three

Our girls were at school, and while Tyler was napping, I was folding laundry in our bedroom, relishing the peacefulness of the sunny, spring day. Usually I would have been watching *The Guiding Light* or listening to Dr. Laura, but now, as I made three piles of the children's clothes, all I could think about was them and how quickly they were growing, presenting me, as a mother, with more challenges every day, challenges I was determined to meet.

On this day, my confidence level was high. I was able to see that Lee and I had worked hard in the last ten years to give them a comfortable, stable home, where they had plenty to eat, nice clothes to wear, and parents who were actively involved in their lives. We had come a long way from those days in that decrepit farmhouse, surrounded by cornfields. Lee had enrolled in the RCIA program at church and was a few short weeks from becoming a Catholic, and he and I had figured out how to enjoy our marriage again, since he was no longer working full time from California. I was happy without consciously choosing to be, and that was unfortunate. Happiness that is not deliberate leaves itself susceptible to attack.

And then the phone rang.

I have since wondered how many lives have been changed by phone calls. I imagine life-altering calls happen every day, maybe thousands of times a day—calls that bring the news of someone's death or illness. And for some reason, when the shrill ring of the phone on the nightstand sliced into my untroubled state, I knew that the temporary tranquility had been a gift, a time of serenity before the ambush, a time of gaining perspective before losing all clarity of thought.

And so I continued folding clothes.

Actually, maybe I unwittingly chose not to answer the phone at the exact time that I shouldn't. God finds a way of telling me all the things that I don't want to know but need to. Maybe if I'd answered, my life wouldn't have changed. Maybe the caller would have hung up. It turned out he was brave enough to talk to the answering machine, but would he have been as courageous or as anxious to destroy us if I had picked up the phone?

"Lee, this is Mike, Stephanie's boyfriend," an unfamiliar voice announced. Perhaps, because I didn't recognize the names, my skin began to crawl. "You need to stop coming out here to California, and screwing around with my girlfriend, and screwing around on your wife, and screwing up my life."

I don't know if that was all he said or not, because I stopped hearing anything at that point. Sinking down on the bed, I was aware of nothing beside the fact that my heart was racing, and I was shaking all over. And because Lee was presently in California on a short maintenance visit, my mind was spinning like the *Wheel of Fortune,* and I waited for it to land on a coherent thought. *Was he with this woman now? Had this been going on the whole time? Was he living a double life? Should I call him? Should I call a friend? Should I climb under the covers and lay there until I died? Death would be good. His death would be better. Should I kill him? How would I do it? Maybe the plane could crash on his way home.*

When my mind came back to the present moment, I realized that I was holding a sock without its mate and felt some satisfaction in knowing that I was not the only one to have been left alone.

CHAPTER

Twenty-Four

I had never called him on the job when he was out of town. I trusted him and did not want to be one of those wives who questioned too much or constantly checked up on him. I didn't think I needed to, but I suppose I should have known I needed to. I had to make a few calls to figure out how to reach him, and then I was put on hold while he was being paged. Someone came back on the line and said they were having difficulty finding him, but they would have him call me once he was located. *Was he*, I asked myself again, *with her?*

I sat on the edge of the bed and stared at the phone while contemplating the end of my marriage. It certainly wasn't the first time I had contemplated it, and it, most likely, wouldn't be the last. And just as I usually did, I told myself that I would be fine, that I was strong and independent.

Only a minute or two passed before the phone rang. Maybe the other wronged party in this messed up situation was calling back to drive the knife into me a little deeper. Maybe it was a solicitor, and I could transfer my anger to the unsuspecting individual who might dare ask me to donate money on the worst day of my life.

But knowing that it was probably the man I now hated most in the world, I answered it.

"Hello," I said, cautiously.

"Hey, Jewel, is everything okay?" he asked.

My, how I hated him! How could he sound so normal, so calm? I wanted to eradicate his composure.

"Well, that depends." I told him. "Do you know someone by the name of Stephanie?"

"You have a niece named Stephanie," he replied. "Is that who you mean?"

"No, I'm talking about the one you've been screwing in California," I said, my voice rising, "the one whose boyfriend just called here and left you a message to stop screwing up his life."

He was quiet. "Julie, there's a girl here named Stephanie," he said. "I've talked to her a couple of times in a Country Western bar, but that's all we've done."

"Well, Mike doesn't seem to think that's all you've done!" I shouted.

"I don't know anyone named Mike," he reassured me calmly. "Listen, Julie. I'm so sorry that you had to get that message. I'll be home tomorrow, and we can talk about this. I promise it'll be okay."

Whether or not it was true, that's what I wanted to hear him say. I would wait to hear him out. I would put off hoping for his demise. Instead I called my friend Stacy, and said, "Hey it's me. I just got a weird call from this guy in California who says that Lee's been screwing around with his girlfriend. What do you think about that?"

"Oh, my gosh, that's crazy," she replied. "Lee's so in love with you. He would never do that."

"Well, I don't know," I said. "I don't think he could do that, but it's impossible to really know another person, and he does a lot of flirting."

"Maybe he does, but that doesn't mean he'd cheat on you," she reassured me again. "He's crazy about you. Have you talked to Lee yet?"

"I called him," I told her, "and he says he knows the girl, but says he's only talked to her and nothing else."

"Then I think you should believe him," she responded.

After we talked a bit longer, I felt better, but when we hung up and I was alone with my thoughts, I started feeling sick again. After all, Lee's behaviors in the past had been questionable at times. He was flirtatious and even more so when he drank. I would be naïve to think it could never happen. *If it turned out it had happened, was I strong enough to end the marriage? Would a strong person stay in the marriage?* I would have to wait nearly twenty-four hours before I could see his face. Maybe his eyes would tell me the truth.

I put the laundry away, and then stared down at my sleeping son, praying that he would be able to enjoy a stable and secure home and family throughout his childhood.

CHAPTER

Twenty-Five

Not surprisingly, sleep did not come easily that night, distracted as I was by troubling thoughts. Just as I had done in the laundromat all those years ago, I tried to guess at Lee's true feelings, motives, and behaviors. I wanted to know the truth so badly, yet I wanted to believe he could never have cheated on me whether it was the truth or not. It turns out I wasn't ready for the truth. God knew I wasn't ready. I wasn't even ready for what I did find out.

"Julie, I might have kissed her," he said.

He had returned home on the late afternoon flight and had spent the evening denying that anything had happened. But when we were in bed, he said, "I might have kissed her, but that's all."

My heart sank, and I put as much distance between us as I could. The edge of the bed felt like the edge of my world.

"We've been talking about this for hours," I said, "and now you tell me you *might* have kissed her. *You might have kissed her!*"

"I'm sorry," he said, but as far as I was concerned, the words were meaningless. "It was no big deal," he went on, rolling over to face me, "but I knew you'd make it one. Are you telling me that, in the eleven years we've been married, you've never kissed anyone else?"

"Are you joking!" I demanded incredulously, jumping out of bed. "No, I've never kissed anyone else. *I'm married*, you idiot!"

"Calm down," he told me. "I know it was wrong, but things happen, and I can't believe you've never even thought about kissing someone else in the time we've been together."

It was easy to see that he was trying to switch the focus to me.

"You are such a jerk!" I screamed. "I can't believe you could kiss someone else and then tell yourself that it's okay because you think I've probably done the same. You know I would never do that to you. I would never cheat on you."

"Oh, that's right," he said. "I forgot. You're the perfect wife. You never do anything wrong."

His face was in the shadows, but I knew if I could see it, it would show no regret. That would come later. In this moment, like many we'd experienced before, he didn't get it. He didn't understand the severity of what he'd done. He didn't know how much he had hurt me. In the war, which our marriage had become, I was temporarily defeated and living in the land of unhappiness.

CHAPTER

Twenty-Six

I didn't know what to think or how to think about myself, my husband, or my marriage. *How was I supposed to move forward, knowing that my husband had kissed another woman? What if he was telling me that he had kissed the woman in California, and it had been more than that?*

I needed to talk to her. I wanted to hear her voice, and I wanted her to tell me she had not slept with my husband. Lee said he did not have her number and all he knew about her was that she worked in a realty agency. I told him to do whatever he needed to do in order to get me a number where I could talk to her.

I knew that if he got me the number, then the possibility existed that he had had it all along, and it was also possible that he would call her and warn her about my upcoming attempt to reach her. On the other hand, if he claimed that he couldn't find it, then there was the possibility that he didn't want me to talk to her, because he was afraid of what she might say.

The next day he gave me the number of her place of employment. He had supposedly found it through calling the Realtors in the area where he had stayed, and he said he did not speak to her. *He was, I knew, probably lying, but what did I expect from such an honest, faithful husband?* Sarcasm comforted me.

Having what I considered to be evidence of my husband's indiscretion in my hand made the situation more real. I stared at the piece of paper and silently called it nasty names. All I wanted to do was hide from this situation and pretend it had never happened. He had been silly to give it to me, particularly since I would have preferred being able to think that he had no clue how to ever reach her again. But now that I had it, I had every intention of using it.

While he was at work, I dialed the long distance number with trembling fingers. "California Realty," a woman answered. "Can I help you?"

"May I please speak to Stephanie?" I asked, making sure not to disclose the fact that I thought Little Miss Stephanie was a hussy who messed around with other women's husbands.

As soon as she came on the line, I hated everything about her, including her quiet, seductive voice.

"This is Julie," I said, "and I believe that you know my husband, Lee. I'd like to know if you slept with him when he was working in California."

"No," she said. Damn that voice was annoying. "We just talked a couple of times."

It was absolutely what I had hoped to hear, even though I knew she could be lying to protect Lee and herself.

"Then why did your boyfriend, Mike, call here and tell Lee to stop coming out there and screwing around with you?"

"I don't know." I could almost see her shrug. "He's not my boyfriend anymore, so I don't know why he did it."

She was so calm and collected that I believed her, although perhaps, it was only because I wanted to so badly. But when I hung up, I didn't bother to say good-bye. After all, she might not have slept with my husband, but she had kissed him.

CHAPTER

Twenty-Seven

Two weeks had passed since the phone call from Mike, and Lee and I continued to be distant. He had apologized several times, but I felt as if I would never want to be close to him again. *How could I trust him? How could I respect him?* I didn't feel as if I had anyone with whom I could talk about these issues. I wasn't talking to Lee, at least not as I normally did. I was close with my family, but we didn't share intimate details of our lives with one another, and I didn't want them to think badly of the man to whom I was, after all, married. Stacy no longer seemed to want to talk about what was happening between Lee and me, so I felt alone in my distress.

I focused on the needs of the kids and tried not to make the fact that I currently didn't like their father too apparent. I prayed about it and figured God would eventually open my heart to Lee again. When he told me that his mother was coming for a visit, I thought God had arranged for her sojourn in order for her to help me love her son again. I believed that if anyone could convince me of Lee's benevolence, it would be her. I looked forward to her arrival and thought about how to approach the subject. *Should I say, "I received a funny phone call"?* No, it was far from funny. *Was it interesting?* Yes, but that adjective had a positive tone to it. I was going to have to consult a thesaurus before her arrival.

When we embraced, I felt comforted. I was fairly certain that Lee had said nothing to her about our situation. He would have been too embarrassed. No doubt then she thought that our marriage was as solid as it had ever been. However, on the second evening of her stay, with the children in bed and Lee having been called back to work for a few hours, I had the opening that I needed to discuss *the call* with her alone. We had been chatting about Lee's siblings and their families when I was aware that God was urging me to say what I needed to say.

"I received an upsetting phone call a couple of weeks ago," I told her. "Some man called here and said Lee's been sleeping with his girlfriend when he's been in California."

Here we go, I thought, *help me to feel better. Help me to believe Lee couldn't have done this.*

But instead, she said calmly, "Sandra always says that all husbands cheat at one time or another."

What! In this, my time of need, when I really needed reassurances, was she really quoting her sister who had been married and divorced five times?

I would have liked to come up with some sort of clever response to let her know how absurd it was for her to quote that woman at this particular time, but I could do nothing but blink and think.

Was I supposed to presume that my father-in-law had cheated on her? Had there been a time when her sister had comforted her with that observation? Had my husband been raised around this attitude and come to believe it? Did this mean that my husband had indeed been unfaithful beyond the kiss?

Whatever the answers to those questions, she had brought the conversation to a screeching halt. Saying that I was tired, I went to bed, wondering if God had heard those words of wisdom from the woman whom I thought he had sent to help me save my marriage.

Later, when Lee climbed into bed, trying not to wake me, I said, "It's all right. I'm not asleep."

"You okay?"

"Not really," I told him. "I talked with your mom tonight. I thought she'd defend you and help me like you again. But do you want to know what she said to me? She said that your aunt told her that all husbands cheat."

He sighed. "Well, maybe you should've told her what you wanted her to say so you could feel better. She probably thought that would help."

"Why would she think that would help?" I demanded. "It means that she thinks it's fine if you've cheated on me. It means that maybe you think it's fine if you cheated on me. Do you think it's okay to be a cheater? Are you a cheater?"

"No, Julie. Look, I'm tired from working all evening. Can we just go to sleep and talk about this tomorrow?"

It was the second time I had had my concerns brushed off in less than an hour, and I was as far from being able to fall into an untroubled sleep as I had ever been in my life.

CHAPTER

Twenty-Eight

As a result of what I had learned in the psychology courses I had taken in high school and college, I had come to think that everyone was basically good, including my husband, who, although he might have kissed another woman, would not necessarily have slept with her. He just couldn't have. I believed to my core that he was too decent and had too much integrity to have engaged in such extreme betrayal. The phone call had been destructive, but it had not killed us. We pressed on, as a couple, as a family, and as Christians.

But then the phone rang again.

Several months had passed since the initial call that had smeared mud on our beautiful family picture. This call came late in the evening, and Lee took it on our cordless phone. After listening for a few seconds, he went into the bedroom, which was not unusual since he often paced while talking. And there was nothing unusual in the fact that he had apparently been notified that he had to go back to work. That had happened occasionally since his assignment in California had ended.

"Okay," I told him. "I'll probably be in bed by the time you come home."

He kissed me before he left, as he usually did.

One might say that I was incredibly gullible, and I suppose that would be correct. But I was also optimistic and faithful, not only to God and my family but to my belief in the goodness of the human spirit. It's also important to understand that in the ten years we had been married, I had rarely caught Lee telling lies, primarily because he did not filter his thoughts. If they came into his mind, then they usually came immediately out of his mouth. I had cautioned him about this many times, as he commented on the weight gain or bad breath of others. He was not the contemplative type who caused me to wonder what he was thinking. So, no, I didn't question where he was going or if he was being honest.

But surprise, surprise! This time, as it turns out, he wasn't being honest, at least not at first. But when he came home, less than an hour later, he sat down on the edge of the bed and said, "Julie, I'm not going to continue to lie to you. I didn't go to work. I went over to Larry and Stacy's, because a couple of their friends are accusing Stacy and me of having an affair."

"What the hell are you talking about?" I asked, sitting up in the bed.

"Well, just listen," he said, clearly trying to soothe me. "Last summer when you got that horrible call, and you were so upset, and I thought I was going to lose you, I called Stacy and asked her to meet me, because I needed somebody to talk to about what was going on with you and me. She and I met at a park and one of her friends saw us and assumed we were having an affair, but we're not, I swear."

"Oh my gosh, are you kidding me?" I demanded anxiously. "And why is this coming out now?"

"I don't know. I guess because Larry and Stacy just got engaged and their friends don't think they should be getting married if she has been with me. But she hasn't. I just want to be with you. You've got to believe me, Julie."

When I got out of bed and marched into the living room, he followed me.

"I have to talk to her and see what she says went on between the two of you. This is absolutely ridiculous. I can't believe I am dealing with more crap from you."

"But nothing happened," he insisted.

"Nothing happened?" I hissed. Angry as I was, I didn't want to wake the children. "Nothing happened except that the two of you went off behind my back together and did who knows what! You are unbelievable."

By the time I was ready to leave, he was sitting at the dining room table, holding his head in his hands.

"I'm sorry, Julie," he said. "I'm so sorry for all the stupid things I've done."

This time, however, I was too angry to even want to believe him. I'd had it with sorry this and sorry that. It was time for me to take action.

When I got to the house Stacy shared with Larry, they were both there, looking tense. I questioned Stacy about what the heck had gone on between her and Lee, and she shared the same story he had.

"Do you believe this story?" I asked Larry.

He didn't answer me, but I saw the pity in both his and Stacy's eyes, and so I left. They pitied me because of my unfortunate marriage to an untrustworthy man. That was when I knew that I had to be alone so that I could talk with God.

What's going on, Lord? I asked Him once I was safely in the car.

"No matter what happens or has happened," I heard Him say, "I am always with you."

I tried to sleep in the guest room, but my mind was racing. *Why did they look at me that way? Is there more to this situation than I have even guessed? Why does my husband continue making horrible decisions? How can I stand living a life where people pity me because of the man I married? How can I move past yet another indiscretion on Lee's part?*

But there seemed to be no answers. Staring at myself in the mirror the next day, I saw a face heavy with agony. And I didn't know the half of it yet.

Section Two—
Death

CHAPTER
Twenty-Nine

That morning, Monday, March 25, 1996, Lee didn't go to work. He said we needed to talk. I agreed, and once the girls left for school and Tyler was playing quietly in his room, I began by telling him that he needed to move out.

"Julie, I know I've messed up again by not telling you about meeting with Stacy," he said, "but that was a while ago, and lately you and I have been in a better place. Can't you see that?"

"What I see is a person I don't know," I told him.

"But you know me," he protested.

"No, I don't, and I don't respect you either," I said. "You lie. You have secrets, and I can't sit around waiting for the next phone call and the next lie that's bound to come because you keep screwing up. It hurts too badly. It's like a punch to the gut. You need to move out."

"Jewel, come on. We can work through this. I love you."

"I believe you do love me, but I believe you love yourself even more, and you always have. You placed yourself in a compromising situation with my best friend. You kissed some woman in California. You're mean and do stupid things when you're drunk. I'm guessing I don't know the half of all you've done."

"Julie, please."

"No, Lee, I can't live like this anymore. You don't get it. You don't understand what your lies and bad decisions have done to me and to us. You can't have lies and have a healthy relationship. You just don't seem to get that."

"Julie, I get it," he said, and I saw that there were tears in his eyes. "I want us to be better. I want to be a better person."

And I? What did I want? More than anything, I wanted to trust him, to forgive him, to move forward. But that didn't seem possible.

"I don't trust you," I said sadly. "I don't think I can ever trust you again."

For a long moment, he was silent, staring at the floor. And then he said, "You're right. I need to be completely honest with you."

I had asked for the truth. And I knew—somehow I knew—that what he was about to say would put an end to everything we had built together. I wanted to run. I wanted to throw open the front door and run down the driveway and run as far and as fast as I possibly could so that his next words would never catch me. I wanted to be anywhere but here where I would have to hear his confession.

Before I could escape into the safe, unknowing outside, he said the words I had been terrified of hearing.

"I haven't always been faithful to you."

At that I lost control. A plastic cup that Tyler had filled to the brim with pennies was sitting on the arm of the couch. I backhanded the cup, and a shower of pennies rained down across the room. Then I began to strike Lee over and over again as he sat unwilling to defend himself.

When I ran into the bedroom, he followed me, and I began to hit him again, beating my fists against his chest.

He grabbed my wrists and held me down on the bed.

"Let me up!" I demanded between clenched teeth, and when he did, I wrenched the beautiful diamond anniversary band he had given me a few months before as a Christmas gift off my finger and threw it at him.

Suddenly I felt as cold as ice. The emotions that had been raging inside of me disappeared.

"Get out," I told him. "Get out of this house and leave me alone."

He turned around slowly and walked out of the room with his head down, shutting the door on his way out.

CHAPTER
Thirty

A couple of days later, the girls and I were making breakfast. As the biscuits popped open with the sound of a gunshot, I knew that they were watching me to see if I would grasp my chest, as I usually did, and gasp, "Oh! They got me!" before sliding to the floor, where I would end up in a motionless heap. This was the signal for them to kneel down beside me and try to revive me with a kiss, whereupon making a miraculous recovery, I would engage in a round of tickling before we returned to our biscuit making. I was aware that they knew today would be different, but that clearly didn't keep them from hoping.

I knew what they wanted. They wanted a sign that I was okay. They wanted a sign that our family was okay. But I couldn't give it to them. I wasn't okay. We weren't okay. I continued to concentrate on opening the biscuits and placing them defiantly on the pan, if for no other reason than to avoid looking at their disappointed faces.

When the silence and tension became too much for her, ten-year-old Nicole asked, "Where's Daddy?"

I still didn't make eye contact. She looked too much like him, and I was too angry. Unable to think past my pain, I retorted,

"Who knows? Probably off doing something else that's ignorant and selfish." And then I shoved the biscuits into the heated oven and went to the sink to wash my hands.

After taking a moment to absorb that statement, she said, "Sometimes you say I'm just like him, Mommy. Am I?"

I had been looking out the window over the sink, and when she asked that question, I felt what little energy I had drain from my body, and my eyes closed. I wanted so badly to escape into sleep, to shelter myself from this sorry life I now found myself in, but I couldn't. If only for these babies that I loved dearly, I needed to be stronger and better. I breathed deeply, trying to fill myself with the energy I needed to carry on. Nicole was so beautiful, even with her blonde ringlets tangled and matted from her night of sleep and a trace of dried milk around her mouth. Even though she often tested my patience and could be disobedient and ornery, I loved her so much. And now she was waiting, her blue eyes wide, for an answer.

"Sweetie, Mommy's sorry for being such a grump," I told her, kissing her on the forehead. "Mommy thinks you're perfect in every way." I hugged her tightly. "Mommy will always love you just the way you are."

I was feeling good about my comeback into the world of the nice mommies until she asked, "But what about Daddy? Will you always love him?"

Tight in my embrace, she couldn't see my face, but because Renee was watching, I managed a smile.

"You know," I said, "speaking of your father, I should probably go and check to see why he hasn't left for work yet. You girls go and get ready for school, and we'll meet back here to eat when the biscuits are done."

As they bounced off to their rooms, I envied their energy and resilience. I, on the other hand, had to take another deep breath before going to the master bath where Lee was getting dressed. Since the massacre of our marriage he had not yet figured out where to go, and he still dressed in that bathroom to disguise the fact that he was actually sleeping in the guest room.

I found him with his back against the wall, sitting on the floor next to the sink. He was half dressed, wearing only navy slacks and a brown belt. His elbows rested on his bent knees, and across his face, he was holding a hand towel. He was sobbing. I was glad.

He sensed my presence and tried to compose himself. When he lowered the towel, I saw a face that was contorted in misery. "I'm so sorry," he said, his eyes on the floor. "What can I do?"

"Yeah, well, there's a hair ball in the sink you can unclog for me."

"If you would forgive me, I would eat that hair ball."

We made eye contact. I noted the sincerity of his statement and his suffering.

I hesitated for only a second. "Eat away."

CHAPTER
Thirty-One

After my initial enraged outburst, Lee's confession had become anesthetizing. I moved around the house as if I had received a full-body, extra long-lasting Novocain injection. My interactions with the children and the outside world were minimal. I lay by the fireplace, on the couch, or in our bed in a nearly unconscious state though, occasionally, I would be overcome with uncontrollable shivering and shaking. By the third day, the stupor began to wear off. I knew I had to pull myself together for the kids, and I had to come back to life even though it meant I would have no protection from the pain of my invisible wounds.

Lee had not been able to return to work. He too lay in bed for hours. As my senses returned, I began to put together a checklist of the actions I needed to take in order to reclaim a life. Getting him out of the house was number one on the list, because I knew I couldn't appropriately handle my hostile attitude with him in close proximity.

"I need you out of this house," I told him accordingly, "because if you aren't, it's possible I could come in here and try to bash your head in with a baseball bat while you sleep."

No doubt it was a histrionic pronouncement, but I didn't care. I wanted to hurt him in every possible way, and sleeping comfortably in our home all day, no matter how depressed he was, scarcely seemed like punishment enough.

"You need to find your own place," I told him.

"We can't afford that," he said. "I've been leaving you alone. Please let me stay until we've worked this out."

"You should have thought about the expense of maintaining two households before you decided to sleep around," I told him.

He had, by now, admitted to several one-night stands during his out-of-town trips over the years, including the girl from California. The very thought of what he had done made me ill.

"Fine," he said wearily. "I'll find an apartment if you really think that's what's best for our family."

"Don't you dare make it seem like I'm not thinking about our family," I told him. "You were the one who forgot about our family. You destroyed us, not me." With that I started to leave the room, then, turning back, I said, "When the kids get home from school, we should tell them that you are going to be moving out."

"Don't you think we should discuss how to tell them?"

"Why? Are you afraid I'm going to say, 'Kids, your dad's a jackass and didn't love us enough to stay faithful, so he's moving out?' Don't worry. I love them enough to soften this for them. It'll be fine. They're already well aware that things between you and I aren't good. They may not be shocked at all."

"So, that's it? We just tell them I'm moving out and hope they're fine."

"Yep, that's it. You're welcome to tell them you're a jackass if you'd like, but I promise I won't."

I had once told Lee that I hated it when he swore, because it hurt my ears. Now I was taking advantage of curse words regularly to emphasize my anger until they had become a staple of my vocabulary diet. Swearing now came more easily than praying. I knew I needed to get back to praying and give up cursing, but like eating, I wasn't making it a priority. Getting back to prayer would be added to my checklist, just after telling the children that their family as they knew it was defunct.

CHAPTER

Thirty-Two

Lee had been left with the impression that I was fairly nonchalant about the discussion we needed to have with the children. In truth, I knew all too well that separation and divorce would disinherit them from the security and stability that all children were entitled too. And this, in turn, caused me to question myself. Could I somehow work through this with him in order to keep the family intact? *No, no, no,* I thought, *I can never forgive such betrayal.* The children would have to be okay. Children survived divorce. My children would survive.

Although there were only a few affordable apartment buildings in the area to check into, Lee had a one-bedroom rented the same day I told him to move out. Lee told me that while asking about availability he had cried in front of the office manager, who was an acquaintance of mine. I was embarrassed and sure the rumor mill would now begin to grind its way through town, but in the big picture that was the least of my worries. What was important was that our children had to be told.

That evening we called them into our bedroom and asked them to sit on our bed so we could talk about something. They had been called in for a bedroom talk only once before, when our dog had passed away, so the atmosphere was tense all around. The children came in quietly; Nicole and Renee side by side as if taking reassurance from one another's presence, and Tyler following close behind, carrying his white seal puppy, named Tuppy. I expected Lee to do most of the talking based on the fact that he was responsible for our situation, but when the kids were settled in the middle of the bed, and I looked to him to begin, I realized that he was crying.

"As you guys might be aware," I began, "Daddy and I haven't been getting along lately and so we've decided that it's best if he move out of the house for a while. He found an apartment and is going to move into it the first of April."

"Is this because Daddy bought the new truck?" Nicole asked, tearing up. "I was the one who told him to buy it. It's my fault, Mommy, not Daddy's."

I put my hand on her knee. "No, baby," I explained, "that's not it at all. This has nothing to do with the truck, and you kids have to understand that you haven't done anything wrong."

I looked at Lee to see if he was going to do or say anything, except hide in his shame.

"I made bad choices," he admitted. "This is all my fault. It isn't because of anything you kids or your mom did. And I'm very sorry."

"Daddy's sorry, Mommy," Nicole cried, climbing on his knee. "Can't you forgive him?"

Renee, more stoic, sat Indian style on the bed, motionless, while Tyler lay on his side, hugging Tuppy to his chest and looking from one person to the next as though trying to understand what was going on.

"I wish it were that easy, honey, but it just isn't," I said. "Daddy and I love you kids very much, though, and we don't want you to be frightened. You will still get to see him. You can go to his place and have sleepovers, and he will still come to all your activities."

After taking blame for what had happened, Lee seemed to have retreated into himself, fidgeting with the string from the waistband of his sweatpants. He was weak, and I despised him for it.

"Are you and Daddy going to get a divorce?" Nicole whispered, wiping away her tears.

"I don't know, hon," I lied, trying to offer her some reassurance. "We're going to see. Why don't you kids go watch television for a little while and let Daddy and me talk, okay? We can answer more questions later if you have any. Just know that we love the three of you more than anything, and we will figure out how to make this situation the best it can be."

I couldn't look at their frightened, heartbroken faces any longer. The more upset they were, the more I loathed Lee for his selfish behaviors that brought them this pain. After I gave each of them a hug, they went to their father, and I could tell from the way they hugged him that they were sorry for him, and that I had become *Mom the Punisher.*

"What the hell was that?" I demanded in a low voice, as soon as they had left the room and closed the door behind them. "I had to do all the talking while you sat there, bawling like a baby, making me look like the bad guy as always."

"I told them it was my fault," he replied dejectedly. "What more did you want me to do?"

"Maybe I wanted you to be the one to tell the kids that their family was falling apart. But, oh no, you had to let me play the heavy while fun-loving Dad gets beaten up again. They feel sorry for you, because mean old Mom is making you move out. Just leave me alone. Please get out of here and leave me alone."

Slamming the door of the master bath behind me, I turned on the hot water, poured in bubble bath, and found a radio station that was playing Shania Twain's "Whose Bed Have Your Boots Been Under?"

It was, I thought, as I began undressing, *a singularly suitable song.*

"And whose lips have you been kissin'," I sang as I yanked my T-shirt over my head. "And whose ear did you make a wish in?"

By the time I had finished the chorus, "Is she the one that you've been missin', baby? Well, whose bed have your boots been under?" I was nude and surprisingly felt a little better. I wasn't the first person this had happened to. I had an ally in Shania.

I slid timidly into the water, and the heat burned off a little more of my stress. However, I quickly realized I had forgotten a washcloth, so I leaned out and across the bathroom to grab one on the towel rack. As I did this, Lee opened the door.

"Oh God," he mumbled as he stared at my body held up by one hand, two-thirds out of the tub, clothed only in bubbles.

"What the hell are you doing?" I demanded.

He covered his eyes with his right hand and said, "Oh, gosh, Jewel, I'm sorry. I knocked a couple of times but you didn't hear me. I just wanted to say I'm sorry for not handling that better with the kids, and for everything. And I'm sorry for walking in on you, but God you look good."

"Well, those others must have looked amazing in order for you to risk losing me to be with them, so go find them and leave me the heck alone!" I exclaimed. I grabbed the washcloth and backed into the tub.

His eyes were still hid behind his hand as he said, "Jewel, they were nothing. I was always drunk, and I don't even remember what they looked like. You're perfect and what I did was stupid. You have to believe me."

"I do believe I'm perfect and you're stupid. And I also believe I will never trust you again, so shut the door and let me enjoy my bath."

He yielded reluctantly, finally saying, "All right," and then backed out of the room, dropping his hand and quietly closing the door, fighting the urge to look at me again.

Actually, I was pleased that he had seen me like that and pleased that it had potentially increased his regret over losing me. The mixture of angry musical performance, nearly scalding bath water, and peep show had strengthened me. I relaxed into the tub and thought, *What can I conquer next?* I considered my checklist.

Tomorrow I would get tested for AIDS.

Then I took the washcloth, put soap on it, and vigorously scrubbed between my legs as Brooks and Dunn began singing "You're Gonna Miss Me When I'm Gone."

CHAPTER
Thirty-Three

Turns out he had told my friend, Stacy, everything he had done. She had been his confidante. She had also been one of my closest friends. They both swore they had not been physical, but they had crossed a line of intimacy with the secrets they had shared. I couldn't call her to go with me to the doctor, nor could I call Shelly since she and John had moved to Illinois. And so I called my friend Janet, who I knew I could count on to be both calm and trustworthy. Like Shelly and John, she and her husband, Steve, had been friends of ours since shortly after we moved to Missouri.

When I explained the situation, she vehemently expressed her sympathy. I abhorred being the object of pity, but at this particular time I appreciated her compassionate nature. She understood when I told her I was too embarrassed to see my primary care physician, so she recommended someone I could see at a local walk-in clinic and agreed to meet me there.

As I drove north on the highway, I assessed my life thus far. I was not yet thirty, I had three children, I had slept with only one man for the last decade, and only two in my lifetime, and I was on my way to get an AIDS test, which was now highly publicized and encouraged due to Magic Johnson's diagnosis a few years before. I had always prayed and loved God and tried to be a good person. I knew that life was not fair, but I wanted it to be fair to me. I knew it could be worse: something could have happened to one of my children. But if I ended up with an STD because he slept around, I would despise him even more for doing this to me.

As I pulled into the parking lot, I was relieved to see Janet waiting in front of the building. I took the nearest parking spot, turned off the engine, and scrutinized myself in the rearview mirror. Although I looked haggard, I felt suddenly inspired. "Here we go, Julie," I said to myself, and it seemed as though I was mouthing God's words, "You can do this."

Once inside I had to fill out paperwork, and my *can do* attitude wavered as I considered how to discuss the symptoms that brought me to see the doctor. I pondered it briefly and then wrote: "No symptoms but need an AIDS test." When the receptionist asked me to sit down, I imagined that she was looking at me curiously.

I sat down heavily next to Janet, and we sat in silence. Infidelity, like death, didn't lend itself to easy conversation between friends. When someone dies we think about our own mortality. When someone cheats, we think of the vulnerability of our own relationship. *Was Janet contemplating her own, I wondered? Was this the wake before the funeral of my marriage?*

"Julie," called the nurse as she held open the door to the examination rooms.

I stood and gave Janet a grimace, then followed the smiling lady in the blue scrubs through the doorway and down the hall. She led me to an empty room where she took my vital signs and then left me alone on the exam table to think about the reality of why I was there. It occurred to me to call it off and walk out. I did not believe I would test positive, but I also did not believe my husband would be a repeater cheater, and I had no way of knowing the slut level of the women he had been with. Considering the fact that he was always wearing his beer goggles, some of them could have been men. I put my head in my hands as that thought coursed through me. I was not accustomed to such raunchy musings, and now they came easily and entertained me in a sick sort of way. I wanted to start laughing insanely, but I was fearful of crossing the border into the land of the mentally incompetent, so I merely chuckled at my newfound sense of lewd humor.

When the doctor rapped and came in, I was so startled that I nearly fell off the table.

"Whoa! Are you okay?" he asked me, his face expressionless.

Had he read my paperwork? How much was he asking with that question?

"I'm Dr. Stevens," he said. "It says on this form that you want to be tested for AIDS? Is that correct?"

"Yes," I declared. "My husband has been unfaithful to me."

The doctor looked about ten years older than me. He was mildly attractive and was wearing a wedding ring. I wondered if he had ever cheated on his wife.

"It's not actually a test for AIDS," he instructed. "What we do is draw blood and test it for HIV, which is the virus that causes AIDS. We'll be testing to see if you are HIV Positive."

I thought his bedside manner left much to be desired. But what did I expect? He was a doctor, not a counselor, and I was a jilted woman with an attitude.

"Well, let's get to it then," I said.

"All right," he said. "I'll have my nurse come back in and draw some blood, and then we'll schedule a time in a few days for you to return for your results. Do you have any further questions?"

I had a lot of questions. *Could my husband love me and still have sex with strangers? Why were so many women willing to sleep with married men? How badly would divorce affect my children? What percentage of women contracted the HIV virus because their husbands were unfaithful?*

"No," I answered.

I needed this to be over. Draw my potentially lethal blood and let me go. The doctor left, and the nurse returned and I stayed silent and safe within myself. When it was over, I hugged Janet, thanked her, and hurried to my car. Once inside, I rolled down the window and took a deep breath of fresh air. I had done it, and it was about more than knowing the results. Following through with the test was a means of proving my strength to myself. I was young, brave, and competent. My life was decent, and I was lucky.

I deserved to go shopping.

CHAPTER

Thirty-Four

Big Lots served as an antidepressant, its only negative side effect being an occasional bout of overspending. Cheap furniture, holiday decorations, toys, makeup, and random food items were mood lifters more efficacious than any medication. I ambled past the couches and kitchen tables and envisioned them in the small, adorable home that I would purchase for myself and the children after the divorce. No longer would I have to put up with dirty work boots or grease-stained clothes. I could be content and successful as a single mother.

I contemplated the items I would buy when I was living on my own but only necessities made their way into my cart: a sturdy laundry basket, shampoo and conditioner, and envelopes. And then I saw what God had led me to find. There, amidst the stationery items of paper, pens, and arts and crafts supplies were the journals, strewn about and stacked unevenly on different shelves, all the same 5x8 inch size. I pulled out a white one with small red polka dots and red and purple flowers on the front and stopped short when I read the title on the cover, "Julie's Journey Journal." I blinked a couple of times to be sure I had read it correctly. Yes, that was what it said. And there were others, including one with a picture of a girl and a duck, and another, featuring two mice dressed in their finest clothing. They were all labeled the same.

After pausing to ask God what he wanted me to do, and deciding that he did not intend for me to buy the entire inventory, I selected five, and then neatly arranged the rest for the other Julies that were on a journey.

My marriage might have been dead, but I certainly was not. I felt very much alive as I left the store and headed toward my broken home knowing that God's presence in my life would continually pull me from the abyss.

.

CHAPTER

Thirty-Five

A few days later, Lee moved out. He loaded a small table and chair, a mattress, a microwave, and a television into our van, his new truck having not yet arrived, and tearfully headed to his new place on the other side of town. Feeling bold and frightened at the same time, I picked out the cutest journal and began writing.

April 2, 1996

It is exactly one week and one day since I learned that my life was never what I thought it was and my life would never be the same again. I am now on the beginning of a journey to a new life, and I am not sure what to leave behind. And because I'm also not sure which direction I should head in, I seem to be stalled at the end of an old life that, while full of happiness, was also flawed with lies.

April 3, 1996, 3:44 a.m.

The anger is keeping me awake. I shiver and try to take deep breaths. I've never felt anything like this. It is so consuming and so scary.

This is his first night in his apartment. I wonder if he is sleeping like a baby. I want to harass him—and every woman who was ever slutty enough to sleep with him.

He was such a good liar, and I was such a trusting fool. I never ever doubted his honesty. In eleven years, I never doubted it. I never knew the human spirit was capable of such cruelty. Or maybe I knew it, but I couldn't fathom how someone who was claiming to love me so much could purposely hurt me so badly.

I think back on so many memories and so many times I should have questioned him but didn't. Perhaps I was in denial. Even when he finally told me the truth, I told myself that it couldn't be true, that he loved and adored me, that he would never risk losing me. I wanted him to take the words back so that I could keep living in blissful ignorance.

Why hadn't he owned up to what he had been doing ten years ago, before we had two more children and so many memories? Memories of cuddling and playing. Memories of kissing and making love. Memories of giving him every ounce of myself, because I loved him with every ounce of myself. And I thought—I truly believed—that he felt the same way about me! I truly, truly believed it, because he looked me in the eyes and told me that he loved me and that I was the perfect woman.

How could one person be so cruel? How could he be so cruel to the one person who loved him and trusted him so completely? *The pain is excruciating!*

I hardly slept that first night he was gone. The fact that he now had the opportunity to sleep with other women was not lost on me. However, I was fairly confident that he wanted to save our marriage and therefore would be on his best behavior. I also felt comfortable in allowing him freedom, because if he was weak enough to sleep with someone during our separation then I certainly didn't want him back.

He called early the next morning to say that he too had hardly slept and that he had put something in the mailbox on his way to work a half an hour before. Although I told him I would get it later in the day when I had to run an errand, I went to get it immediately. It was a note on a small piece of paper:

> I'm not sure what to say. I love you, miss you, and want to be with you. I don't want to go through life wondering if you are okay or my kids are okay. If we aren't together, we won't know how the other is doing. We have a great family, and if we solve some problems, we will be stronger. Please don't give up. It will be worth it. It's all in God's hands.
>
> I Love You,
> Lee

He now used God to his advantage whenever possible. The man had gone from "Who's God?" to "God can save us and our family!" I was confused as to whether I should be angry at him for being a hypocrite or praise the Lord, because Lee was being saved. My thoughts ran amuck regarding my marriage, Christianity, and the morality of my husband and the world.

I had asked him whether he had slept with anyone since joining the church a year ago, and he had said, "No, but why does that matter?" Why did it matter? Maybe it didn't, but I felt better, believing my husband had joined the Catholic Church and then had not allowed himself to cheat on me again. That is, if you don't count him sneaking around with my best friend.

Due to this situation and the fact that my moral compass was now askew, I considered sleeping with her fiancé, Larry. An undercurrent of mutual attraction had always existed between the two of us, and I wondered if having sex with him would help me feel better. I was tired of always being the person who tried to do the right thing. I didn't want to let God down, but I also knew He would forgive me, as He does all sinners who repent. I felt justified as I drummed up the courage to call him and ask if I could come over and talk.

As I drove over there, I told myself I was merely getting a male perspective on my situation. I wanted to know what he thought about what Lee had done. I wanted to know if there were repercussions for him and Stacy. And I wanted to know if I could cross a moral boundary as Lee had done.

I don't remember much of what we talked about when I got there. I just recall knowing that I couldn't sleep with him, even though he told me that the reason Stacy wasn't there was because they had called off their engagement. *Lee and I were separated. It wouldn't have been that bad, right?*

Wrong.

It would have made everything more complicated than it was already, and it would have turned me into the kind of person I could never allow myself to be if I wanted to call myself a Christian. I couldn't help wishing that Lee had been so enlightened.

CHAPTER

Thirty-Six

And so, the fact that I couldn't cheat when we were separated made it even more difficult to understand how Lee could have cheated when we were doing okay.

"My counselor believes it's all tied to alcohol," he told me when I asked him to stop over and talk after his first counseling session on April 3. "That's because I only cheated on you when I was drunk."

"What does that mean for us?" I asked. "I've wanted you to give up drinking for years, and you've never even been willing to consider it."

"This is different, Jewel," he told me earnestly. "I've never been truly afraid of losing you before. I've never had to live in a crappy apartment by myself before. If I have to choose between alcohol and you, I pick you and this family every time."

"I don't believe it," was my response, but imperceptibly the top row of bricks from the immense wall that I had built around myself began to tumble down.

"I know it's going to take time for me to prove it to you," he said, "and I'm willing to give you all the time you need."

Up until now, I had been confident that our marriage was over. But now I began to wonder. *What if? What if he really does give up drinking? What if he really does become an amazing Christian man because of this experience? What if we can work through this and never fight about other women or alcohol again?* But then my sense of self-protection kicked in, and I asked myself what would happen if he did it again. *Once a cheater, always a cheater, right? I'd be an idiot to even consider taking him back.*

But what about the kids? Did I owe them an attempt at working this out? They were so confused and so innocent. That same morning, Tyler and I had run an errand. When we returned, I asked him to pick up his toys, and I went into the bathroom. When I came out, he was standing in a corner, his face in his hands.

"Whatcha doin', big man?" I asked, kneeling down beside him.

He dropped his hands and turned to me with a tear-stained face.

"If I be bad like Daddy, will you make me move out too?" he asked.

I dropped to the floor and pulled him gently onto my lap.

"Baby boy," I said, giving him a big bear hug, "Mommy will never make you move out. Mommy's sorry that you are hurting and sorry that Daddy has to live somewhere else right now. I know it's scary for you, but I promise I will not make you move out until you're all grown up and begging to live on your own. Mommy and Daddy love you so much and never want you to be afraid."

I kissed him on the cheeks, forehead, and nose until finally he smiled. Then I started singing. "I want some baby back, baby back, baby back. I want some baby back, baby back ribs." He started squirming and laughing, because he knew I was going to begin nibbling on his back and chewing softly on his ribs. I munched on him as he wiggled and giggled, completely forgetting the tears he had shed only moments before.

It occurred to me that it would be nice if someone would nibble on my baby back ribs and make me forget.

Lee would be willing.

But that, I told myself, *is not, as far as I am concerned, even a remote possibility.* Our playful days were over. I could never forgive him, even for the children's sake.

CHAPTER

Thirty-Seven

On Easter weekend when we celebrated the fact that Jesus died for all of us and then rose again, I admit that I could think of little else beside my overwhelming desire to punish and humiliate Lee. I wanted him to openly admit to both of our families what he had done; therefore, regardless of the fact that it had only been a couple of weeks and it would require many hours in the car together, I stuffed my anger, and we followed our usual routine of traveling first to be with his family and then spending time with mine.

At his parents' house, we were able to talk alone with his mother while the children slept early Saturday morning. No doubt she had sensed the tension between us, as Lee looked so worried, and I had been so quiet when we had arrived the night before. And when, over coffee, he began to cry, it was only natural that she should want to know what was wrong.

Let's be honest. As much as I loved her, I wanted to put some blame on her. Her attitude of "all husbands cheat" had probably been instilled in my husband as he grew up. Of course, this probably wasn't true, but given my current state of mind, I thought she should have been clearer about what was right and what was wrong and made him more aware that infidelity was unacceptable. But it was too late, and it didn't do any good to take fault with her at this point in time.

Finally, Lee spoke up. "I've made some choices I'm not proud of," he told her. "I've been unfaithful to Julie, and I've moved out of the house and into an apartment."

Her first reaction, just as I might have guessed, was to ask me if I couldn't just forgive him.

"It wasn't only once," I argued defensively, "and I could have gotten a disease or he could have gotten some other woman pregnant. It's just not that easy."

She looked at me as though she didn't understand. *Did that mean that she had or would have accepted it if his father were unfaithful? And if she had, did that make her a better person than me? Did it mean she was stronger than me? Or weaker? Why was I questioning myself?*

"Julie has every reason not to forgive me," Lee said. "What I did was unforgiveable."

He was right, and I left it at that. I couldn't make any promises or give her false hope. Her son had messed up in a profound way, and I wished she would have been able to acknowledge it, even though, as the mother of a son myself, I could understand her desire to support him. What I didn't understand or expect was my own family's support of him.

"I've made some mistakes, and Julie and I are separated," Lee told my parents in their kitchen later that same day.

My father's response was to throw his hands in the air just the way he had when I had told him I was failing physical education in the ninth grade. What I was afraid to tell him then was that the grade was the result of my not going to tennis practice, because I had a fear of asking him for a ride home. What I was too afraid to say now was that I needed him to be supportive and not angry and disappointed. But, once again, I was afraid to speak out and tell him the truth, to say, "My husband screwed around on me, and you're angry with me?"

Later, when we were alone, and he asked me how long I was planning on punishing Lee, I knew it was futile to hope for compassion from him. My father wasn't coldhearted; he was old-fashioned and Catholic. And it occurred to me that he may have been unfaithful to my mother, which would explain his apathy and her reticence.

But I was in no condition to think about that.

The sympathetic nurturing that I did not receive from our parents came, not surprisingly, from my heavenly Father when I went to church that weekend. Entering the wooden pew and kneeling before the large crucifix on the day that Jesus rose from the dead was like coming up to breathe after being under water for two weeks. I was safe, understood, and accepted once again. I was saved, and along with Jesus, I would rise from this deathly place that I was in.

"People may let you down, but I never will," I heard Him say.

Closing my eyes, I linked my fingers together in prayer: *Dear Lord, I am so angry, and I am so hurt. Even in Your house, I wish pain upon him as he sits at the other end of this pew. I grit my teeth as I remember once again what he has done. What he has done is unforgiveable. Maybe not to You, but it is to me. I am sorry, Lord, because I cannot be Your perfect servant. I am human, and I am weak and I am broken. Please heal me and guide me. Be with me and the many who suffer more than I. Thank you. Amen.*

I felt His love and approval, but I also began to hear His gentle urgings, "Did you not say 'For better or worse'? Did My Son not suffer more than you? Did he not forgive his offenders?" I wanted God to guide me, but I wasn't sure I was ready to ask those questions of myself. I reminded God that the Bible named adultery as the one reason to justify divorce. *And wasn't my husband a confessed adulterer?*

When our family rose with the rest of the congregation for the gospel reading, I found it difficult to focus on my blessings and the miracle of Jesus rising from the dead, because somehow all I could think of was the prodigal son who had come home after fornicating and riotous living. I knew God was welcoming Lee with open arms while I, who had not broken His commandment, felt as though I were in the wrong. It wasn't fair.

I leaned forward to look past the relatives who separated us, and I saw on Lee's face a serene, not quite smug look. Since going to confession, I knew he was joyous in his newfound freedom from his sins. I was not. I was tortured. He caught me looking at him and smiled a small, apologetic smile. I quickly inched back and refocused on Jesus on the cross. *If Jesus could die to save the world, could I allow my feelings of fear and pride to die in order to save my family?*

When it came time for the *Our Father*, I took Nicole's hand and held it tightly while we recited the familiar words.

"Our Father, who art in heaven, hallowed be thy name. Thy kingdom come. Thy will be done on earth as it is in heaven. Give us this day our daily bread, and forgive us our trespasses, as we forgive those who trespass against us…"

Wait. Hold up. Did I ask God to forgive me like I forgive others? Am I required to forgive Lee, if I am to be forgiven by God? What the heck?

I vaguely heard the priest invite the congregation to exchange a sign of peace, and then those around me began turning to shake my hand. I was somewhat numb to it all and do not remember who I hugged or whose hand I shook. But I do remember seeing Lee blowing me a kiss, and for a moment, my frozen heart seemed to melt a little. *What was wrong with me?*

And God said, "Nothing is wrong with you, my child. Nothing at all."

CHAPTER

Thirty-Eight

Before we returned home from our Easter visit, I needed to see one other person. I called Lee's best friend, Joe, who had been the best man in our wedding and asked if I could talk to him. Leaving Lee wondering where I was going, I drove to Joe's house. He didn't ask any questions, so I figured he must have some idea of what was going on between Lee and me. I wondered what he knew and who he'd heard it from. I remembered a game I had played as a child when a group of us sent a whispered message down the line and laughed to see how the final message differed from the original. Perhaps Joe had heard that I was the cheater, or perhaps he thought Lee had moved out, because he was in a new relationship. Most likely he had spoken directly to Lee at some point in the last couple of weeks and had a fairly accurate picture of what was going on between us. Joe and I had become good friends over the years, but I'm not exactly certain what I had hoped to gain from going to see him.

When I told him about the separation, he was sympathetic, but when I asked him if he had known about what Lee had been doing, he hedged until I became so upset that he had to be open with me.

"He knew it was wrong, Julie," he said.

"*Really?*" I waited for him to lock eyes with me, and then I continued. "He knew it was wrong, yet it happened over and over again? I don't get it, and I need someone to help me get it. You are his best friend. Please help me to understand how he could do this to me?"

I was begging him to tell me something, anything, that would help me feel better, but all he said, putting his hands on my shoulders, was, "I'm sorry, Julie. I really am."

"Well, I'm sorry too," I retorted, standing up to leave. "I don't know why I came here. I'm sorry to bother you."

I felt like a fool. The whole world pitied me. I was pathetic. I cried in the car as I drove back to my in-laws. When I got there, I went straight to the bedroom to gather my belongings so we could return to Missouri. I was shoving my clothes into my suitcase when my father-in-law walked in the room. Tears were running down his face as he opened his arms to me. I accepted his embrace. I appreciated it, because it was not given with the expectation that I forgive his son. I was not pathetic. I was reminded once again that I was loved, that I was strong, and that I would eventually feel happiness again.

CHAPTER
Thirty-Nine

Also on my checklist was individual counseling, because I was still looking for answers, and I thought perhaps a therapist could assist me in gaining greater understanding. My anxiety was high as I sat in the waiting area and thought about sharing my husband's infidelities with a complete stranger. I was embarrassed because my situation was embarrassing, but I knew I needed help I wasn't getting elsewhere—I needed professional help, as did Lee. He was seeing someone else in the same office.

When the therapist called my name, I was startled and jumped from the chair to follow her. We walked down the hallway and entered a small, neat office that had a desk, a bookshelf full of books, and a few soft chairs. Next to my chair was an end table that held a lamp and a glass bowl of peppermints. Because my eating had been sporadic, and oftentimes nonexistent, I had a persistent case of halitosis, so I grabbed a round, hard candy and slipped it in my mouth, as she explained the counseling process and the limits of confidentiality.

And then she asked, "So what do you need to talk about today?"

I swished the peppermint around in my mouth and replied, "My husband has been unfaithful to me."

With that said, the candy slid down my throat and became lodged.

I interrupted her response, whatever it was, and asked rather hoarsely, "Could I have a glass of water?"

The water forced it down a little further, so I could breathe properly, but it was still causing pain in my chest, and it so disconcerted me that I ended up saying very little, and I imagine she found me curiously unresponsive. At any rate, she ended by suggesting that Lee and I go to couple's therapy, and when I did not protest, she scheduled the appointment herself.

It was no surprise that I did not find my first experience with counseling particularly encouraging.

A few days later, Lee and I went to couple's therapy, although I must confess that I was expecting little more than to enjoy the pleasure of witnessing the embarrassment he would undoubtedly feel as I recounted his numerous vices to the mental health expert. Individual therapy for me, even if it had helped, didn't seem fair. Lee needed to be present and hear my pain in order for it to feel therapeutic.

This time a male therapist escorted us back to his not-so-orderly office. The numerous bookshelves regurgitated books, and the desktop had not seen the light of day in a very long time. Furthermore, the room was stuffy and the air was stale. Lee and I squeezed into a love seat together, and the counselor, who sat in a comfortably aging arm chair across from us, explained that he had spoken with our individual counselors and he was aware of our situation. Next, he asked if he could get some background from each of us about our childhoods.

"Julie," he said, "I'm curious about your relationship with your father."

"My dad?" I questioned incredulously. "You want me to tell you about my dad?"

"Yes. Could you please talk to me about how the two of you got along? Were you close? Did he ever yell at you or spank you?"

"He was great," I responded defensively. "He hardly ever got mad at me, and I remember being spanked only a couple of times, but it wasn't a big deal."

Suddenly I realized that for some inexplicable reason I was crying. I grabbed a Kleenex from the nearby box and dabbed at my eyes and nose. Lee remained motionless by my side.

"What's causing you to become so emotional while talking about your father?" the therapist asked.

"I don't know," I said. What I did know was that I didn't want to talk about my dad. What I did know was that this therapist thought we were getting somewhere because of my tears, but the somewhere I wanted to get was right out the door. I wanted to talk about my marriage. I wanted to talk about my husband's behaviors that had brought us to this messy place. Talking about my dad wasn't going to get Lee and me anywhere fast.

I was angry when we left at the end of the hour, angry with the therapist and angry with Lee, who gave me a half smile as we walked out, which I interpreted as satisfaction on his part that we had not talked about all his misdeeds. I understood that the therapist wanted to use our pasts to help explain the present, but because it had upset me so much, I considered it psychoanalytic bull crap. Psychoanalysis was an appropriate form of therapy for some people, but in my mind, it was not effective for an initial marriage counseling session in which infidelity had occurred. I wasn't going to forgive my husband by processing any past resentments or disappointments, which were, as far as I was concerned, completely beside the point.

Truth was, I would have resisted a counselor of any therapeutic persuasion if he or she didn't agree with me that Lee was the perpetrator of our problems. I was the victim. I was the innocent. I was the Christian.

CHAPTER

Forty

"People who are not in some kind of pain do not commit adultery."

That was a quote from the book, *Adultery: The Forgivable Sin* by Bonnie Eaker Weil (1993). Because the couple's counseling had upset me so much, I bought this book only to become enraged by this sentence, which appeared on the fourth page of the introduction. *Was the author joking? Was I supposed to believe and forgive Lee, because he was "in some kind of pain" when he stuck his penis in other women? Really? Really?* I read no more.

The counselor and the author were not necessarily wrong, but they were wrong for me. It had been less than three weeks since I had found out, and the only words that caused me to consider forgiveness were those of God, my children, and Lee.

The voice of God and His expectations for me to forgive and love unconditionally were like an annoying shadow, ever present and unwilling to leave me unattended. It followed me everywhere. When I picked up the Bible, it opened to Luke 6:37, "Do not judge, and you will not be judged. Do not condemn, and you will not be condemned. Forgive, and you will be forgiven," and went on to say, "A good measure, pressed down, shaken together, and running over, will be poured into your lap" (NIV). I wanted good stuff poured in my lap. I imagined if I could forgive Lee, then God would fill me with unending joy. I certainly wanted that, but to receive the good measure, I would have to stay married to a man I couldn't trust and didn't respect.

God's message was not restricted to the Bible. I heard Him through Sunday sermons, daily calendar quotations, and songs. On the country music station to which I regularly listened, a song entitled "If God Can Forgive Me, Why Can't You" was played with disconcerting regularity.

> I've smoked a little pack and I've drunk a lotta gin,
> And I've even been down to a house of sin,
> The things I've done I can't undo,
> but if God can forgive me why can't you?

I didn't particularly like the song, but I did believe it was a message God wanted me to hear.

Meanwhile, the children were sending me the same message. Renee, in particular, was a constant reminder of the efficacy of forgiveness. "Everything's going to be okay," she would tell me, flashing a crooked-teeth grin whenever I was upset.

"How do you know that, Lou Lou?" I would ask.

"Because I pray about it, Momma," she would tell me confidently.

Her faith was inspiring to me, but also scary. *If I couldn't forgive and reunite with her father, would she blame God and give up praying?*

She also expressed confidence that everything would be all right in a letter that she sent to Lee.

> Dear daddy, I love you so very much. I herd mom say on the phone that you were so sweet. I just know you and mom are

going to get back together. Thank you for being so nice to mommy so that you can get back together again.

Love your daghter, xoxoxoxo
Renee xoxoxo

෨

Nicole was confused and kept trying to figure out what her father had done that was so terrible. It occurred to me that she might have a clue when she asked me to list the Ten Commandments because, she said, the only one she could think of was, "Thou shalt not covert [her word], thy neighbor's wife."

"What," she asked, "does that mean?"

"It means that a man shouldn't take someone else's wife," I hedged, hoping to end the discussion. Lee had told me that at least one of the women had been married, and the reminder sent me into a rage. *What type of woman does something like that? How immoral would she have to be to cheat on her spouse and with someone else's? Are people like me who can't imagine being so selfish the minority?*

"What's the greatest commandment of all, Mommy?" Nicole was still looking at me inquisitively, and I realized I needed to stop the ruminations and focus on my daughter. But it was so difficult.

"Well," I told her, telling myself to get it together for her, "um, I think God wants us to love him above all else and with every part of us."

She thought about it for a few seconds. "Does that mean we have to love each other, since God created all of us, and we're all a part of Him?"

I wondered if God had put her up to this. *Why did she have to ask so many questions and such hard ones?* I didn't want to respond, because I knew she was trying to tell me that I needed to love her father, no matter what he did.

"I guess that's what it means, honey," I conceded. "But it's not always easy to do."

We smiled at each other reassuringly, and I found myself feeling as though I were the child, and she the mother.

❧

Tyler got right to the point. "I'm mad at you," he told me one morning when we were driving home from the YMCA, where I had tried to improve my mood through exercise.

"Why did you make Daddy move out?"

"Daddy and I agreed it would be a good thing for us, because we weren't getting along," I told him. "I'm sorry that it hurt you and made you mad at me."

We drove in silence. He was my best little buddy, and because I didn't want him to be upset, I asked him if he was just a little mad at me.

"No," he said. "I'm this mad." And in the rearview mirror, I could see him spread his arms as wide as they would go. I didn't think my heart could be broken anymore, but I could feel his outspread limbs tearing the wound even deeper and wider. I hated Lee for what he had done to this family. I drove the rest of the way home with clouded vision.

Once we were home, and I unbuckled him from his car seat, we both began to cry.

"Mommy's so sorry, baby," I sobbed. "Mommy's so, so sorry."

"Mommy," he said, "can I ask Daddy for a sleepover tonight?"

What was I to do? I hated Lee, but I loved my children. My love had to be greater than my hatred. "We'll talk to Daddy," I reassured. "We'll ask him."

I knew what the answer would be.

❧

Listening to Lee was a magnetic experience for me, one which I tried to resist. He said he was a changed man. He said he believed in God. He said he wouldn't turn away from God again or me and the kids. He said he wanted to renew our vows and start over.

After the children had gone to bed that night, he told me, over and over again, that he loved me, sounding like a man who had recently been released from prison, and I could tell that he felt free of sin and guilt. He had confessed to God and to me, and he was, as he sat beside me, rugged, handsome, lounging by the fireplace, clearly comfortable within himself.

I cannot lie—it turned me on. A new improved man had taken over my husband's body, and I was having sensations like I had never had before. He reached out to touch my face, and then scooted toward me, slid his hand behind my neck, and rested his forehead on mine. Our eyes were closed, but every other part of my body was open to a flood of powerful feelings. And then there was the familiar scent of him, Old Spice deodorant mixed with Tommy Hilfiger cologne.

"I'm so sorry, Julie," he whispered. His breath was hot against my cheek. I knew I had lost all sense of self when I leaned into him and our mouths met. I wanted him to kiss me, really kiss me, and I wanted him to touch me. I wasn't doing him any favors. I was doing this for me, to satisfy my own unrecognizable desires. I let out a small groan as our tongues met. It had never felt like this before. My body ached and throbbed as he ran his hands up and down my back. I felt as though I was awakening from a long sleep.

But when I started to go further, he took both my hands in his.

"No, Julie," he said with a groan. "Don't."

His self-control and my lack of it was more than I could take. When I fell against him, exhausted and tearful, he wrapped his arms around me and held me tight. I was still trying to figure out what had happened when he asked me if I was angry with him for putting a stop to it.

In reality, it was the sexiest thing he had ever done, but I simply said that I was going to bed.

"Okay, Jewel," he said as I pulled away from him. "But don't forget that I love you."

Pretty words.

They were such pretty words.

CHAPTER

Forty-One

My body had betrayed me. There was no other explanation for what had happened. My body had tricked my mind into thinking I wanted to be kissed and touched. But how could I possibly want to kiss the lips of someone who had kissed others during our marriage. But the feelings I had experienced had been absolutely amazing and totally unexpected. The next morning I couldn't reconcile with my desire for him.

The words of our parents had the opposite effect. Unbeknownst to them, they pushed me away from Lee and stirred up my angry stubbornness. My father had written me a letter after our Easter visit, making excuses for Lee, who, he reminded me, had been so young when we had married. Lee was, he said, such a hard worker and had always provided for me and the kids. He brought up the subject of my children and how they were suffering, as though I hadn't already considered it. And he mentioned that I came from a line of forgiving women, whatever that meant. These arguments were not as upsetting as his suggestions that I not expect Lee to change completely and to make a decision now rather than waiting any longer.

He meant well, and I lost no time in replying, addressing the letter to the entire family and not just to him.

> I know all of you have been thinking about us and praying for us. I apologize for not writing or calling sooner, but I am spending all my time trying to heal and to figure out what direction I want my life to take. I want to do what is best for the kids, for myself, and for Lee.
>
> I received Dad's letter, and I know he thinks I need to make a decision, and I know what decision he wants me to make. I, too, am hoping that Lee and I can work this out, but I have to be sure that we are both willing and able to take our relationship to a new level, one that is based on complete honesty, total respect, and unmistakable love. I am not willing to settle for anything less than that.
>
> Each person is only given one life, so being in a relationship where there is only some honesty, respect once in a while, and love only when the mood is right is not acceptable. I do not want my children to settle for that; therefore, I do not want them to see me settling for that either.
>
> You raised me to be a very confident, strong, and mature person. I want to be with someone who also has those qualities. I want to be a wife to my husband, not a mother who fixes and forgives everything when he decides to act like a child.
>
> I know that Dad thinks I am being too hard on Lee and that I shouldn't expect him to change completely, but I have faith in God and faith in myself that if Lee is not willing to go the distance for me, then I am fully capable of going it alone.
>
> Lee was not the only one who was young when we got married. I was very young and scared to death, but I worked hard every day to be a good wife, a good mother, and a good

person. Lee did not do the same. He let his love for himself come before his love for me and the kids several times. I will no longer accept that, and whether or not he is capable of changing that pattern is yet to be determined. Right now, he is willing to try, and because of that, I am hopeful.

I want nothing more than to keep this family together, but we have to be happily together. Lee and I have gone through some life-altering experiences, and we are both different because of it. We have to get to know one another again, and that takes time. We are being patient, and you must be also. We appreciate your thoughts and support and encourage you to continue praying for us. God will show us the way. Thank you for being the family that you are!

Love always,
Juliene

I tried to express kindness, honesty, and respect. I had other thoughts that I didn't write, such as the forgiving women I descended from didn't have other options. My mother couldn't drive a car or write a check. Her circumstances forced her to be dependent on a man, and I never would be. I also questioned why the men I had descended from couldn't have been men of integrity who didn't need forgiveness. But I couldn't write all that, because it would have been hurtful to everyone concerned.

I heard through others that my mother and his mother thought I was pushing Lee too far and they were afraid he was going to walk away. I thought, *Let him walk.* His ego got us into this situation and mine was not going to get us out of it too quickly. I had too much pride to readily forgive and possibly too much to forgive at all.

Lee told me that a coworker of his had said that I should either forgive and give our marriage a chance or just get a divorce. This coworker was married to the woman with whom he had cheated on his first wife. I told Lee if that was the kind of person he wanted to listen to and the kind of advice he agreed with, then we could call the attorney. He said he didn't necessarily agree, but that I had to be realistic and stop, as he put it, "trying to live in a fairy tale."

"If I'm going to be realistic, then I have to file for divorce, because at this moment, there is no way in hell that I can ever forgive you for what you have done," I told him. "It is the fairy tale side of me that causes me to believe we could come out of this better and stronger. Which do you want?"

He decided he liked the fairy tale side after all.

CHAPTER
Forty-Two

I wasn't completely ignorant of the blessings in my situation. My husband was fighting for me, instead of leaving me, and he was groveling a good deal of the time. My STD test came back negative. None of the other women had shown up at the doorstep escorting an illegitimate child. My children were healthy, and every day we lived in the comfort of a nice home with plenty to eat. In a moment of thankfulness and weakness, I agreed to go on a date with Lee.

On a beautiful, crisp spring night, he knocked on the door and then walked into the house wearing his nicest collared shirt and jeans. He had gotten a haircut, was freshly shaven, smelled delicious, and was wearing a broad smile. I leaned against the dining room table as I stared at him.

"Hi," he said shyly. As long as we had been married, I could never remember my husband seeming bashful, but on this night he appeared tantalizingly timid. I vacillated between reminding myself that I should hate him and feeling like I could definitely love this man again. I was allowing my senses and not my good sense to encourage feelings of goodwill toward him.

"Hi," I said in return with a reluctant smile. "Did you want to say hello to the kids before we go? They're playing in the backyard."

He stepped out onto the deck and yelled, "What's goin' on back here?"

I listened to their shrieks of "Daddy," as they raced to join him. The girls reached him first and wrapped their arms around his waist, squeezing so tightly their eyelids scrunched closed while he patted their backs and kissed the tops of their heads. When Ty finally caught up to them, Lee reached down, grabbed him under the arms and threw him up into the air before catching him in a big bear hug. They all laughed together, and, for a moment, I felt as though I were an uninvited guest at their party.

No doubt, sensing my discomfort, Lee said, "Your beautiful mom has agreed to go on a date with me. What do you think about that?"

When they all expressed enthusiastic approval, he said, "You guys have a great time with Ashley while we're gone, and I promise to come in and see you later before I go back to my apartment, okay?"

They all agreed, and he and I left a few minutes later after giving last-minute instructions to the kids and their sitter regarding bedtimes, food options, and not taking a bath in the hot tub after playing in the mud as they had during her previous visit.

"I need to stop at the store and pick up a couple of thank you cards, if that's all right."

"That's fine," he replied. "You know we can do whatever you want."

Once at the store, he occupied himself with picking through cards that talked of love, loneliness, and forgiveness as I searched for just the right thank you sentiment, only to be interrupted by him reading some of his. "A marriage is two people who discover that more and more their happiness is found in one another," and, "Forgive me—forgive me for my faults that seem to follow my life." It was hokey, but it was working. I was melting into him as

I read the sappy words. We were reveling in the closeness of one another, and the sexual tension was so palpable that I rushed to make my choice and get out of there.

But not apparently in time, because back in the car, he turned to me, grabbed my hand in both of his, and asked, "Would you like to see my apartment?"

When I didn't smile, he realized that I had become uncomfortable with the flirtations and knew that I had remembered what he had done.

"I'm sorry, Jewel," he said. "It was a bad joke."

"It's okay," I said, trying to bounce back. "Actually I think you just want me to see how pathetic it is so that I'll let you move back home."

It was obvious that he was thankful that I had decided to joke about it, but then he said something completely unexpected.

"Would you like to stop in at the church on our way to the restaurant? We could pray for ourselves and for our family."

What was there for me to say but yes?

⁓

The Saturday evening mass had just finished when we arrived, and, after dipping our fingers in the holy water and making the sign of the cross, we genuflected before kneeling at one of the front pews.

Be with us, Lord, I prayed, and I asked God to truly enter Lee's heart and allow him to be changed, to be better, to be for real. I pleaded that God help me to be capable of forgiveness. And as always, I prayed for our children, our families, our friends, and for those who suffer. Then I wondered what Lee was praying for. *Did he finally know how, when, and what to pray for? Could he love God and me and the kids more than himself from now on?* I thought skeptically, reminding God that I had good reason to be cynical.

When Lee's arm slid around my waist and he drew me closer to him, I did not pull away. Instead, we leaned into one another, and I let my head fall onto his shoulder. The recent trauma and mental chaos were momentarily replaced with peacefulness. Maybe we had gone through all of this so that Lee could be saved. *Could I trade my pride for his salvation?* Again I heard God remind me, *Christ gave his life for yours.* And then the possibility that Lee was counting on my forgiving him made me so uncomfortable that I suggested we leave.

"Can we light a candle first?" he asked me, and I didn't know how to respond. *How should a wife respond when her husband suddenly behaves in ways she's only ever dreamed of?* I watched him light a votive and close his eyes in prayer. And in that moment, he seemed more like a child preparing to blow out birthday candles than a man engaging in a Catholic ritual.

When he was finished, he opened his eyes and flashed a serene smile at me before reaching out to take me in an embrace. We stood there, holding one another, truly holding one another, for the first time since D-Day: him not wanting to let go, me unsure as to what I was or should be doing, but liking it. It was a surreal moment, surreal and bizarre.

☙

When we got back to the house, Nicole and Renee were already in bed. We tucked Tyler in, and I went into the kitchen and sat on a barstool, where, unlike the sofa in the living room, I was less likely to lose control. But when Lee began stroking my hair, I closed my eyes and let myself relax. And when I felt his lips on mine, we began kissing passionately, and I felt his hand slide under my shirt to touch my bare skin. It was incredibly arousing. But then I reminded myself that this was something he had done with other women. He had touched them and they him. And it had been just as exciting for both of them.

"Stop!" I whispered, my eyes suddenly flooded with tears. "You have to go."

And when he did, I laid my head on my arms and wept. Happiness was a bird that had flown away from me.

CHAPTER

Forty-Three

Confusion, anger, sadness—I was awash with emotions, the majority of them negative. And that was unlike me. But that fact led to more anger, because I believed I had been a good wife. I remembered all the thoughtful, loving moments I had shared with Lee over the years. When we lived in Pennsylvania, I had planned a special getaway for the two of us to the Pocono Mountains. For his ten-year college reunion, I had surprised him by planning for us to return to Kirksville, Missouri, and making arrangements for him to have a day off from work. And then there was the time I had secretly trained to run a 5K with him, even though I detested running. I wasn't naturally a wild and crazy girl, but at times I had tried to step out of my comfort zone and be one for him, because I wanted to be all that he would expect in a wife and mother. I thought it would keep him faithful. I was wrong. I resented all that I had ever done for him and wondered how often I had offered some sort of kindness directly after he had been with someone else. The occasion of his thirtieth birthday, when I had greeted him naked in the kitchen at three in the morning particularly haunted me. Yes, he had appeared to be generous and thoughtful at times, as well, but now I wondered if he had been driven by guilt, whereas I had been driven by love. I heard God telling me that I shouldn't regret acting out of love, but I couldn't help but regret it all.

In April, Lee turned thirty-three. He referred to it as his "Jesus year," since it was the speculated age at which Jesus had died. I didn't plan any surprises, and I was not particularly enthusiastic about taking the children to the mall, where they picked out a cookie cake and a George Strait CD. Lee pretended to be surprised for the kids' sake but later told me it was his worst birthday ever. Since our recent date, I had been back to asking a lot of "Why?" and "How could you?" And I had little sympathy for his birthday party woes. He deserved being miserable on his birthday. He deserved to be miserable for the rest of his life.

I was again focused on myself, my hurt, and what I needed to do for me. The checklist showed some progress: AIDS Test—check, write in journal and get back to praying—check, tell our families—check, see a counselor—check, check. Next, I had decided that I wanted to return to school and get my master's degree. I believed that knowledge and education equaled power, and I wanted to feel powerful. I wanted to feel valuable. And if I were to end up a single parent, I wanted to have options.

With this in mind, I applied to a Master of Science in Education program with the intention of becoming a high school guidance counselor. I was not new to the college application process, but I was concerned about my ability to be accepted without the expected two years' teaching experience. I was required to submit my career plans and philosophy of education. It went something like this, prefaced by an excerpt from a Garth Brooks song entitled "Change":

> "And I hear them saying you'll never change things
> And no matter what you do it's still the same thing

But it's not the world that I am changing
I do this so this world will know
That it will not change me."

As a young girl, I would dream of growing up and somehow saving the world. I believed that I would, someday, be able to make bad people good and sad people happy. I dreamed of delivering such a powerful message to the world that people everywhere would want to spread peace and love. I am a grown woman now, and my naivety has left me, but my desire to help others has not. I realize now that I will not make big changes to this world, but I also know that I cannot allow the cruelties and sufferings that this world inflicts upon me and others to change who I am. I believe in helping others, and I believe in the power of education. I believe that by continuing my education in the field of guidance and counseling I can better equip myself to make positive changes to the outside world, no matter how infinitesimal.

I intend to use a master's degree in guidance and counseling to work in the school system as a counselor or continue being educated and licensed so that the opportunities for me to help others can increase as my own knowledge and abilities expand. I feel confident that the education I receive will enable and encourage me to continue on my journey toward letting the world know that it will not change me. The world may not be saved by my efforts, but I will know that I have tried to make it better.

Some people have asked me why I want to go back to school. They think the education I have is enough, and they see the entire process as a hassle. I see it as empowerment. Life experiences teach many lessons, but education helps one to evaluate those lessons and not only use them to improve one's own life but use them to provide assistance and guidance to others. That is my ultimate goal. I want to do the work that God has called me to do, and I can do it to the best of my ability if I continue to be educated.

The letter was sent to the office of admissions, but the message was meant for Lee and the rest of the world. I was not going to allow my hurt to change who I wanted to be. I would not turn my pain toward the outside world. Instead I was prepared to help others even more now that I knew suffering of my own.

Believe me, I still wanted revenge, and I sought it in a couple of ways. I knew a friend from church that gave massages—in his home. I scheduled one, and it lasted nearly two hours. It was fantastic, and it drove Lee crazy. "He's just trying to get a cheap shot of my naked wife," he insisted.

My lack of response prompted him to ask, "Were you naked? Did he see anything?"

"Of course I was naked," I said, shrugging. "And I don't really care if he saw anything. My eyes were closed, and I was in heaven."

Lee had a pained look on his face, and it made me want to laugh. "Well, he didn't massage your breasts did he?"

"The chest has muscles, too." I hesitated. "But no, he didn't touch my actual breast."

"What about your ass? Did he rub your ass?"

I let out a heavy sigh. "With all you've done, I can't even believe you are asking me these questions."

At that, the topic was dropped. I had made my point and tasted retaliation.

I also went out with a friend on a Saturday night and came in after two in the morning. She was an acquaintance who met Lee's approval because, although her husband had cheated on her, she had remarried him, not once but twice. Not exactly what I considered to be a good example to follow, but I was curious to hear what she might have to say. She and I went to dinner and shared infidelity and alcohol stories. She believed that if the alcohol had led to the unfaithfulness and it had been recurrent, then Lee was most likely going to need professional substance abuse treatment. I wasn't sure. I wanted healing to be easy. I wanted to go back to a time when infidelity had not clogged my thought drain, a time when I wasn't planning my dinner companions based on the commonality of having pathetic partners.

After dinner, I suggested that we go on to a bar and have a drink, but she said she would pass. I had never gone to a bar by myself unless I was meeting someone, but after driving her home, I parked in front of the Letterman's Club and said a prayer. *Lord, I may be acting foolishly and I may regret this decision, but I'm going to do it anyway, and I ask that you be with me and forgive me if it is wrong. Help me to be safe. Amen.* I was a rebel and my cause was to show my strength and independence to myself and my husband, but I needed and wanted God to watch over me as always.

The place was packed with people and foggy with smoke, so it was fairly easy to make my way unnoticed through the noisy crowd to the bar where I ordered a Fuzzy Navel. The dance floor was bouncing to Vanilla Ice's "Ice Ice Baby," and I fought the temptation to join the dancers, because I was alone. I decided I could stand anxiously and awkwardly at the bar sipping my one drink for the next couple of hours, or I could enjoy the atmosphere and eventually dance, but it was going to take the perfect song. Thankfully, "Word to Your Mother" segued into "Macarena."

The girls and I had done the line dance to this song a few times at home, so after sucking up a little more liquid confidence, I slipped into the crowd of dancers and joined them. As I did a hop, turn, and clap, I noticed that a man at the bar was watching me and found that I didn't mind at all. *Let him look*, I told myself. Maybe the fact that my husband couldn't be faithful to me didn't mean I was undesirable.

"Pump Up the Jam" replaced "Macarena," so I was heading back to the bar, when the man who had been watching me, appeared beside me and yelling, "I'm Tom," whirled me back onto the dance floor.

Any further attempts at communication would have been futile, so we danced to that song and then the next and then the next. I'm not exactly sure how many songs we danced to, because I was lost in the music and movement. I was enjoying the attentions from a stranger and the distraction from my real life.

We danced until closing time, when I avoided what might have been an awkward moment by saying that I had to go home, and I was pleased when he not only scribbled his telephone number on a napkin but gave me one of the roses that decorated the tables.

I couldn't remember the last time I had been out so late. Lee was staying with the kids at our house having another sleepover, and I found myself hoping that he might have been concerned about my whereabouts. I wanted to give him a taste of his own medicine, and it turned out that it had worked.

The light in our bedroom was on. He was sitting Indian style on the floor by our bed, and the Bible was spread open on his lap. His eyes were wide and bright with fear.

"What are you doing?" I demanded, throwing the rose and the napkin on the dresser.

"Waiting for you," he told me. "Where on earth have you been? I'm a nervous wreck."

I wanted to laugh out loud. Perhaps I did. How many nights had I waited for him, feeling just the way he did now?

"You deserve it," was my glib response. "Now could you please go to the other bedroom so I can get ready for bed?"

"Julie, what's going to happen to us?" he asked me. "I can't stand living like this. I don't like not knowing where you're at and what you're doing. I want us to be together, and I want to make up to you for everything I've ever done wrong."

"Can we talk about this later?" I said. "I'm exhausted."

"Yeah, I guess," he replied reluctantly, and getting to his feet, glanced down at the rose and the napkin on which Tom had scrawled his number.

"Listen," he said. "I don't ever want to be with anyone else again, and I don't want you to be with anyone either."

"We don't always get what we want," I reminded him and stared him down.

When he left the room without another word, I knew that I had won.

But it wasn't long before he got what he wanted. At the end of April, I let him move back in. Looking back, I know it was too soon, but at the time, he had been told that he could get out of his lease without any penalties, because someone else wanted to move into his apartment. Our finances were tight and we didn't have money to waste. More importantly, though, I couldn't stand to see my children sad or listen to them beg for him to come home. They sang his praises and recounted the ways that he was different. And I could see that he was different – better. He was more peaceful and more excited about God and church. If he was going to be an amazing, Godly person, I couldn't let someone else have him.

I also got what I wanted. I was accepted to graduate school.

Section Three—
Resurrection

CHAPTER
Forty-Four

He was different. We were different. He paid attention in church. He sang along with the choir. He wrote me notes on a daily basis, sometimes a couple of times a day, notes that told of his love for me and for God. He was patient with the children and with my rollercoaster of emotions. He frequently held my hand and gave me small gifts, such as a single red rose or a copy of *Chicken Soup for the Soul*. As a couple, we prayed together on a regular basis, we lit candles, and we read together, the first book being *Love for a Lifetime*, which my sister had mailed to us. In the evenings we enjoyed listening to Yanni and George Winston instead of turning on the television. I had, incidentally, given up soap operas since my life had become one. And we communicated about everything, our fears for the future, and my anger about the past. He also was unwavering in his determination not to drink, and he exhibited saintly restraint regarding intercourse.

Some women only dreamt of being pursued the way that I had been over those several weeks. Yes, the cost had been high. Time would tell if my investment would reap a big return. As he moved back in, I was excited one minute and angry at myself for allowing it the next. We did not share the same bed, but we were under the same roof, and I loved it and hated it at the same time. One night in early May, I went into his room. Since his return we often talked late into the night. On this particular night, he was lying with the sheet, half-covering him as I sat on the side of the bed, unable to think of one more word about the issue that had not already been voiced. I was beginning to resign myself to the fact that the *why* question would never be answered in a satisfactory manner. As much as I hoped to hear that he had only done what he had done because a member of the mafia had held a gun to his head and threatened to destroy the world if he did not follow through with cheating on me, I knew it was too late. Instead of asking him again, I decided to answer the *why* question in my own head, *Because he was a selfish moron. Because he could. Because slutty women invited it. Because I wasn't enough for him.* That last answer spurred me to prove myself as a sexual woman and as a woman worthy of being well-loved. So, when the conversation didn't happen in that warm, silent bedroom, I could feel my body opening up to the idea of redemption.

My eyelids were heavy when I looked at him lying bare-chested, head resting on the pillow. In his gaze, I saw desire fused with fear. He didn't trust my moods any more than I trusted his fidelity. But I wasn't going to allow myself to think of his unfaithfulness as my body yearned for gratification. I was going to show him and myself that I was as desirable and sensual as any woman could be.

Our eyes were linked as I leaned down and our lips met. I was overcome with a craving that was unfamiliar. I had often made love out of a sense of duty. In fact, one of Lee's complaints had been that I had never initiated sex. If our marriage were going to survive, my attitude would need to change. I would have to view sex differently and be more aggressive about what I wanted and needed; the pain had changed me, and brought with it bitterness too great to allow me to play the shy, reserved, Catholic girl role anymore.

I had spent my entire adult life being a wife and a mother, neglecting my physical needs as a woman, because I was bashful and hadn't seen it as important. *I was supposed to make sure everyone else was taken care of, right? Everyone else needed to be okay, before I could ask for something for me or expect my needs to be met, correct?* Well, not anymore, because my sacrifice had not been returned in kind.

I rolled beside him and pulled off my T-shirt and pushed down my shorts. He watched me, visibly shaken, as I undid my bra and tossed it to the floor and then slid out of my underwear. And because he appeared to be afraid to make a move without my invitation, I slipped under the sheet and felt his heart thumping wildly against my breasts. And all this time, he didn't say a word, which was unusual, to say the least, since he could be annoyingly talkative during sex. But now he seemed almost too afraid for words, nearly too afraid for anything, and I found that I liked the quiet dominance that was mine as I lay naked next to him for the first time in well over a month.

He turned onto his side toward me, and we were kissing once more. His trembling hand ran along my thigh and my hip, and then my stomach. My breath caught in my throat, interrupting our kiss. The lightness of his touch and the apprehensiveness of it elicited electrifying sensations. I hooked a finger around the top of his boxer shorts and tugged them off. When we were both completely naked, we lay motionless, staring into each other's eyes. *Had we ever looked at one another with such intensity before?* I couldn't remember experiencing a moment like that. *Had we ever truly made love?*

Without breaking our visual bond, he passed his hand nearly imperceptibly over my breasts. Our eyes still locked, he touched me and I touched him, pulling him toward me.

"I want you," I insisted.

"Are you sure?" he questioned nervously.

"Yes, I'm sure."

We again locked eyes as he moved over me. We had a reprieve from our problems. I lost all sense of time and place as I let the wave take me away into oblivion, rising and falling like the ocean. Our bodies convulsed in unison and then relaxed. We were exhausted and clinging to one another. I held tightly to my husband. I held onto the one who had betrayed me.

Without warning, tears began to fall, and suddenly, I was sobbing in his arms, weeping for all that we had lost only to find it, oh so briefly, again. I wanted to wail aloud because I realized as I pushed myself away from him that I would never be able to experience this pleasure without smelling the stench of infidelity afterward.

"Julie," Lee said, pulling me back into his embrace, "I hate myself for what I have done to you and to us. And I wouldn't have confessed to you if I wanted to continue doing that. I swear to you that I don't want to live that life of secrets and stupidity anymore. You are amazing, and you are all I will ever want from here on out, I promise. I promise to spend the rest of our lives making it up to you."

"But I don't trust your promises," I sobbed. "And I don't trust you. But I also don't know how to be without you and not be a family."

I let him hold me as my tears subsided, but when I whispered, "Maybe, just maybe, we can find a greater happiness together than we've ever had," there was no response.

Lee was already sleeping.

CHAPTER

Forty-Five

We marched for Jesus. Life goes by quickly, and life changes quickly. A scarred and damaged family, we walked the streets of my hometown in Illinois, celebrating with other Christians the goodness of God. The morning of May 25, 1996, was spectacular. The sun was shining, the temperature was mild, and flowers were blooming in the yards of the historic homes that we passed, Lee carrying our son atop his shoulders and the girls bouncing along beside them. Two months prior, our family would not have been participating in this event. But we were changed. We were more thankful for having one another than we had ever been before.

The children were grateful that their parents were living in the same house again and sharing the same bed. I was grateful that the children were so happy, and that I was on my way to becoming emotionally whole again. As for Lee, he had a lot to praise God for. He had been given a second chance with his family, and he had developed a love for God.

Our lives had changed in so many ways. Lee and I also took a trip alone together a few weeks later to Eureka Springs in Arkansas, my head in his lap as I napped during the five-hour trek. He had arranged for us to go to Bonny Brooke Farm Atop

Misty Mountain, a twenty-acre mountaintop property with five romantic cottages. We had reservations at the Barn Rose, described as a vintage barn, reborn with a glass wall looking out over the mountain peaks and valleys. It had a trellised deck with a porch swing and, on the inside, was a queen-size bed and waterfall Jacuzzi. It was private and peaceful, and it would have been perfect if we had been perfect or even close, but we were still awkward, and I was still wounded.

However, I was looking forward to seeing *The Great Passion Play*, an outdoor production of the passion of Jesus, which Lee had arranged for us to go to the second night of our stay. The first night we went to dinner at a lovely little restaurant with an outdoor patio and live music. Lee held my hands across the table and, instead of allowing himself to be distracted as he used to do, focused on me to the extent that our waitress actually asked us if we were newlyweds.

"Hah! Are you kidding?" was the response that came immediately to mind, but I voiced in a mild tone, "No, not hardly" and gave her a smile.

Dinner was enjoyable. Then we drove around the area to see what else it offered. There were quaint shops and inspiring exhibits, and overlooking the area was the unmistakable Christ of the Ozarks Statue. The monumental seven-story figure resided at the top of a mountain, his imposing image standing out brightly against the night sky. As we drove back to our cottage, I could not get his alabaster image out of my head, and I looked forward to seeing him again when we attended the play on the following evening.

Back at the Barn Rose, Lee put Yanni on the CD player, and I started filling the Jacuzzi tub. I added bubble bath, but it didn't look like anything was happening, so I added some more. We helped one another get undressed and stood in a silent embrace for a moment. The laryngitis, which had begun to afflict him just before we left home, had turned out to be a gift of peacefulness.

He wasn't asking if I was okay or if I needed anything. He wasn't talking about what a great job he had done of planning our getaway or what a turn on my body was. He was hushed, and that was a turn-on for me. It played up my growing belief that he was a changed man, now the strong, high-principled, silent type.

We haltingly lowered ourselves into opposite ends of the steamy bath, reclining back once we adjusted to the nearly scalding temperature. He pushed the button for the jets, and the bubble bath that had disappointed, now demonstrated what it could really do. Within moments we could no longer see one another. Bubbles had climbed over our heads and up our noses and in our ears. We swatted at them, spit them out, and brushed them to the side trying to see one another but gave up and gave into the giggles, before turning off the jets and relaxing into our bubble blanket.

The soothing water smoothed the edges of our awkwardness. He began massaging my right foot as it lay on his chest. *So what if he had hurt me in the past?* I thought. *Now I could be spoiled for the rest of my life.* I moaned as he moved his hand to my calf and worked to loosen my tight leg muscles, and I relaxed, more than willing to let him pamper me, and so he did, massaging my neck and shoulders, pulling me close to him, telling me that he loved me. And I tried not to think of how he had hurt me. We were going to be better than ever. I could do this.

But in the end, I couldn't. The sex should have been wonderful, but I felt as though I wasn't fully there, and afterward, I cried. I cried when the sex was good. I cried when it wasn't. *When was I going to be able to find myself again?*

The next morning we walked a trail on the acreage with the property owner's black long-haired dog serving as our guide. Misty Mountain lived up to its name as a light fog spread itself softly across the dark green hills. Branches cracked, and leaves crunched as we made our way through the maze of trees, weeds, and wild flowers. The brush was so thick in places that different species of trees appeared to be married and meshed as one: the oak with the pine, the maple and the spruce trees curled around and intertwined with each other. *If they could hold onto one another through their differences and through the wind and rain, couldn't I do the same with this person who was so unbearably different than I?* I reached back for his hand. He easily joined with me and said sincerely, "Thanks," his voice a little louder than the previous day. My simple gesture was like water for a thirsty Lee.

We ventured deeper into the woods; the smell of earth was strong in our nostrils, and the day crept toward balminess as the hot sun sought us out through the breaks in the trees. Just as God created a variety of people, He had also given us a variety of places, and this Arkansas territory was unique and wonderful in its mountains and natural beauty. Even though Lee had forsaken me, I knew that God had not. He had given me numerous gifts, and this beautiful earth was one of them. In thanksgiving to God, I would try harder to die to self and live for Him. Momentarily exalted, I turned and kissed Lee. When I stepped away, he was grinning from ear to ear.

Peacefulness and tranquility hung with us throughout the afternoon. That evening we arrived at the *Passion Play* early. The seats of the large outdoor amphitheatre looked upon an open, dirt area and stage. I knew the story that we were about to see enacted. I knew it well, and I breathed deeply to strengthen my emotional dam. I knew my heart would break as the people chanted for Jesus's death. I knew my breathing would falter each time Peter denied him, and I knew my teeth would clench when Judas betrayed his Savior, just as I knew that my heart would celebrate when the tomb was found empty. I was fairly certain that Lee, for one reason or another, would not feel the emotions as strongly. But he had brought me here, and he was trying.

The theater was crowded, but a hush fell on the audience as the play began. The production was done beautifully and was replete with live sheep, donkeys, and turtle doves. As I expected,

I was moved to tears when Jesus, in his humanness, cried out to God before breathing his last breath. I felt humbled, because he had died for me, and for Lee, and for each of us, and we didn't deserve it. I was selfish, and yet God chose to forgive me. As Jesus ascended into heaven, I should have been joyful, but instead, I was saddened by my own imperfections and those of every other living human being. I could tell Lee was disappointed by my melancholy mood as we exited the theatre. He knew it meant I was mad at him again, and he was right.

"I'd like to sit on a bench in front of the Christ of the Ozarks Statue. Is that all right?" I asked, knowing full well that he would do whatever I wanted.

Even though Christ of the Ozarks appeared to be dressed in a milk carton, I was still drawn to him. The way his arms were straight out was suggestive of the Crucifixion; however, I chose to see it as him beckoning me to come to him as a parent would his child. His wide arms invited me to run to him with my problems and my pain. I gazed up at him and thought about the hurt that I could not let go of. I apologized to Jesus for my failings and those of the world, and then we left.

We didn't make love that night. We lay in bed together, but we were miles apart. My sleep was restless, and I dreamt that Tyler was killed in a car accident while staying with Lee's sister. As soon as we got up, we tried to call them to ensure that he was okay, but no one answered. We also tried to reach Lee's mom, but again no one was at home. I prayed that my baby was okay and told myself that I needed to trust God. We checked out of our cottage and went to church in Eureka Springs as we had planned.

During the mass, the choir sang my favorite hymn, the song that I sometimes sang to the children before bed: "Be not afraid, I go before you always. Come, follow me, and I will bring you home." I fought back tears, hoping that it was a message that our son was fine as Lee gripped my hand. He knew I was frightened that something could happen to one of our children, and he knew I was frightened of him and the hurt he had caused me.

"How about we do a little shopping before we head out of town?" he asked as we were walking to the truck after church, no doubt hoping that some retail therapy would lift my spirits. "Maybe we can find something to take to the kids and maybe something for Juliene," he added, grinning.

"Maybe," I said.

As long as we'd been married, I'd regularly trapped him in relationship purgatory, the land where he knew not whether I loved or hated him, regularly using apathy as a defense mechanism when I was fearful or resentful.

We drove to a strip of shops that advertised cheap souvenirs and picked out matching T-shirts for ourselves that had "Eureka Springs" embroidered in colorful letters across the front. Then I grabbed three giant lollipops for the kids while he looked through baseball caps stacked on a shelf.

"I think I'm going to get one of these, okay?" he asked.

"Sure," I said. It was unusual for him to buy something for himself without my suggesting it first, but this was, I reminded myself, a new Lee, a fact he confirmed when he joined me on the shop porch, wearing a cap which proclaimed, "Christ is Life…the rest is details."

"Whaddya think?" he asked, sitting up straight, tilting his head, modeling it with pride.

I grinned at him and shook my head from side-to-side.

"What?" he questioned. "You don't like it?"

"I like it," I said, "but who…are…you?"

He looked at me quite seriously for a second and answered, "I'm nobody. Who are you?"

The memory of our poem brought tears to both our eyes. We stared at one another. "Are you nobody, too?" he continued, as he slid closer to me and put his arms around me.

"Then there's a pair of us," I said.

We sat quietly on the bench, nuzzled up, pondering our past, our present, and our future. When I pulled back after a minute or so, he kissed me ever so sweetly and softly. *I could get used to this,* I thought. This was a miraculously intimate and peaceful moment.

We eventually left the bench, the souvenir shop, and Eureka Springs. Lee had planned a stop on the way home at the Precious Moments Chapel in Carthage, Missouri. I was not a collector of the Precious Moments Figurines, but he knew I would enjoy touring the gardens and seeing the chapel. We took the free tour and were inspired by the hand-painted murals and elaborate stained-glass windows; however, the innumerable faces of wide-eyed, round-faced children covering the 9,000 square foot space made me yearn to talk to my son, and so I placed a call to Lee's mother's house from a pay phone.

"Is Ty there, and is he okay?" I asked her.

"Sure. Do you want to talk to him?"

But when I heard his voice, I was so overcome with emotion that I handed the receiver to Lee and ran into the restroom, sobbing. My baby's voice was all I needed to put my life into perspective. The hurts I had suffered were manageable as long as my children were healthy and safe. I was thankful. I praised God's goodness and appreciated God's blessings in my own life. When my tears finally ceased, I blew my nose, washed my hands, and rejoined Lee, who was waiting for me anxiously. I smiled at him, linked my arm with his, and led him out of the chapel.

"Are you okay? Does this mean you're ready to go?" he asked.

"Yeah, I'm okay, and I'm ready to go. Let's go home and be a family."

The circumstances of the infidelity had not changed, but I could choose happiness. I knew now that I could choose my family. I could choose to wear my wedding ring again.

CHAPTER
Forty-Six

At times I still wondered if I should end the marriage. Throughout the summer of '96, there were days when it was easy to choose to be happy and other days when it was not. Even the movies we watched seemed to hold a message for me. *Something to Talk About* with Julia Roberts and Dennis Quaid, about a woman who, with the encouragement of her family, is able to forgive her husband who has been having an affair, made me happy. But *City Slickers*, during which Bruno Kirby asks Billy Crystal, who plays a married man, if he would engage in "the greatest sex in the universe" with another woman, providing his wife would never know, infuriated me, because Crystal replied, "No. I would know." I didn't understand why my husband could not have been a person with that much strength of character.

We took the youth from our church on a trip to Oceans of Fun in Kansas City. Lee raced the kids on the waterslide and interacted joyfully with them throughout the day. When we took a group photo, he held up our sign that read "Soak up the Son." It was easy to choose happiness on that day. But the day we went to the YMCA to work out and he ogled another woman with considerably larger breasts than mine, I actually took off my wedding ring and put it in my shoe with the hopes that someone would hit on me in front of Lee. No one did.

On the days when we made love, and it was mutually satisfying, I was happy. On the days when we had sex and it was all about him as it had been in the past, I was angry.

That summer was full of ups and downs and some in-betweens, but looking back, I remember it as a time of growth and change for all of us. The children had become aware that their family structure was fragile and that their lives had the potential to change unexpectedly in significant ways. They were more conscious of their own behaviors, and they tried not to create stress that might negatively impact their parents' marriage. While Nicole continued to be headstrong, she was more likely to apologize and take responsibility for bad behaviors, such as the time she admitted to spitting on a boy who lived in the neighborhood. Renee wrote frequent notes that praised our parenting: "You're the best parents a girl could ever want. You're the sweetest and nicest parents I know." And Tyler would sometimes wedge himself between us if we sat side by side, and put his arms around our necks, pulling us together. The kids wanted to keep the family boat from rocking as much as they could.

I felt each day that I didn't jump ship was a day of growth for me. In order to stay in the marriage, I had to grab onto my lifejacket of faith and trudge forward. Education also served as a lifeline for me as I began graduate classes and saw my confidence rise and my options increase. Lee kept the boat afloat by patching over the holes that his behaviors had created in the past. He didn't take out-of-town trips. He helped around the house by vacuuming, cooking and cleaning, and he worked with me to plan a family vacation to Disney World, something he would have never spent the money on before. We took the trip near the end of the summer, and invited his mother to come with us.

"Who wants to go to Disney World?" we asked the kids once we had the plans solidified.

"We do!" they responded in unison as they jumped up and down and hugged each other.

We would go to Disney World as a family, and I would be glad I stayed in the marriage to see the delight in my children's eyes as they boarded a plane, took a ride in a teacup, and shook hands with Mickey. Lee and I flirted with one another on the flight and passed notes across the aisle. I wrote: "Lee, I know who you are, and I'm going to like you anyway. I have to like you if I am going to like myself. We are alike—there is a pair of us. Let's be friends!"

Lee passed me a note that he had composed with Tyler's assistance. It had Mom written on the top of the page and then two columns listing my advantages and disadvantages, according to which, although I was pretty, smart, fun to be with, and had nice legs and hair, I was too far away. I wondered whether or not Lee, at least, was singling out my attitude toward him and not just the distance between our seats.

We stayed in a nice hotel. We bought a four-day park pass. We gave each of the children money to spend. We ate out every meal, and one evening we went to a luau at Disney's Polynesian Resort. It wasn't an inexpensive trip, and I feared, with each swipe of the credit card, that Lee's inner-ticking financial worry bomb was going to detonate, spewing out curses and complaints, but it didn't happen.

Interestingly enough, it was Tyler who caused the blast of anger that must have been building inside of Lee. Near the end of the trip, Ty was more interested in playing the Nintendo in the hotel room than he was in getting dressed and ready to go to the theme park. After asking him to put the game down several times, Lee grabbed the game out of his hand, and, telling him to get his ass in gear, stormed out of the hotel room angrily.

Well, there you go, I thought, *he hasn't changed at all.*

I had hoped to never witness one of his temper tantrums again. I suppose I could have given him a break due to the fact that he had gone so long without cracking, and Tyler had been noncompliant, but I didn't feel Lee deserved any more breaks. My tolerance board was all pegged out. I marched the children—Tyler beside me, his hand in mine, the girls behind us, and Lee's mother behind them—down the hallway and through the lobby to the parking lot where the rental car was parked. Out of the corner of my eye, I had caught a glimpse of Lee sitting in a chair in the lobby, and I knew he would follow. Inside the car the purgatory period, to which Lee was well accustomed, began.

I had read once that fear was the reason behind anger. I figured that made sense to both of us.

CHAPTER

Forty-Seven

Lee's admission of sins had included the revelation that he had cheated on me during the summer before we got married with a friend on whom he had had a crush in high school, a young woman whom I had come to know when we lived in Fort Madison. In the fall of 1996, we ran into her at the Catholic Church, and she had happily approached us and gave us both a hug. At that time, the anger and hurt had not yet absorbed into my cells and changed me. I still worried about what other people thought, and I still wanted everyone to like me. I regretted that hug.

A few years later, I saw her at one of the class reunions and, no longer caring whether or not she liked me, did not hug her, in an attempt, whether she knew it or not, to make it clear that I knew what had gone on between her and Lee fifteen years before.

I felt God encouraging me to forgive, and I heard him telling me that we are all sinners. *I hear you, God, and I think, for the most part, I have forgiven her, but I want her to know that I know. And I want her to feel some shame.*

It occurred to me that if all the women of the world, all my sisters in Christ, would band together and vow to never sleep with someone else's husband or boyfriend, husbands and boyfriends would not be able to cheat. I made my own personal vow to that effect.

CHAPTER
Forty-Eight

"Love is a decision." That was what the banner on the wall read. I stared at it and contemplated the meaning of the words until Lee's bouncing knee made it impossible for me to focus. I placed my hand on his leg and gave it a little squeeze to let him know his fidgeting was bothering me and heard him say, "Sorry," just as a middle-aged couple appeared at the front of the room and welcomed us all to the Worldwide Marriage Encounter Weekend.

For ten years, I had asked Lee to participate in one of these weekends with me, and he had always refused. But this time it had been his idea, and as was true with nearly everything he did these days, I was simultaneously pleased and angered. *Why had it taken a nearly failed marriage for him to realize that we needed to take steps to save our relationship? But all that aside, was it possible that love was a decision? Could I decide to love him, infidelities and all, for the rest of our lives?*

Today I could. Today I could look at the anxious man beside me and say that I would try. I would work with him to examine our lives together, and share our feelings, frustrations, joys, disappointments, and hopes for the future. I would allow God to work in us and through us, trusting that He would lead as He always has done.

"We would like to ask that everyone share with the group your spouse's most endearing quality," the man announced.

Yuck. That was not how I had hoped this would start. Lee and I shared a look of dread.

Funny, but all I could think to say was that since my husband had cheated on me, he had no endearing qualities. Thankfully, the words, "He's a loving father," came out of my mouth when my turn came around.

Lee said something about my belief in God and love of family. As the other couples spoke, I feigned interest, because I kept thinking about how difficult this weekend was going to be if this was the approach these people intended to take. My bitterness continued to get the better of me on a regular basis. I had to remind myself that was part of the reason for coming on this weekend and that I could only hope to let go of the past. And pray.

The weekend consisted of this sort of presentation, alternating with sessions in which we were given questions to answer, followed by discussions. We also wrote letters to one another, exploring our feelings about the relationship: feelings, feelings, feelings. I was tired of feeling sad and angry. I didn't want to *feel* anymore. The first evening, while Lee showered, I curled up in a ball on the hotel room bed and bawled like a baby. I had no greater understanding of our situation on this day than I had seven months ago when I first found out the truth. But God was not going to give me understanding. He was going to give me the grace to forgive and decide to love again. I could *decide* to love again, but it was going to be difficult.

We took notes throughout the weekend, and on Saturday I noticed that Lee had written at the top of one of his pages, "God does not make junk!" *Did his self-esteem need that reminder?* I didn't ask.

On the last day we were invited to write a letter to our spouse answering the question: "What are my reasons for wanting to go on living?" Lee wrote the following:

Dear Juliene,

My reasons for wanting to go on living are endless. There are so many things I need to do yet. There are so many things I need to make up for. There are so many things I truly enjoy now.

As you know, I have always loved life. Even though I have moaned and groaned a lot, down deep I can't complain. I've been very fortunate because of the blessings that I have been able to enjoy. Despite making some wrong choices along the way, you are the most right choice I have ever made. Without a doubt, you are the best thing that ever happened to me in thirty-three and a half years. No Question!

At this point, I need to prove to myself that I can be a truly good person, in the purest sense of the word. I know I have the capability of doing this, and I need to live to do it.

I also have a need to make things right with you and reach a higher plane with you. I know we can do it. But only through the grace of God will this be done. That is a very strong need that I have to repent and give something of myself back to the community. I don't want to end this life as a failure. I have a need to improve myself. I want to learn patience. I want to learn how to give you and the kids unconditional love.

I want to go on living for you, in order that we can be great together, because that will affect so many lives, mostly our children's. You are a great person, not perfect. I am a great person, not perfect either. Together—and you know this is true—we are awesome. Ask anyone. We affect people in truly positive ways. I want to continue to do that. We complement each other perfectly. We are two halves of a whole. The bottom line is that we have a lot of unfinished business together, and I want to start or continue right away.

We've experienced some extremely low lows. It's time for us to experience some really high highs, all the time, not just once in a while. I have an incredible desire to love you all the days of your life. I enjoy many things in life. However, none as I enjoy *you*!

Our marriage, although it has encountered some rough waters, has been a truly great experience. You wrote how much you loved me and wanted to spend your life with me. You also wrote about how much I've hurt you, and I respect that feeling too. This weekend has given us the time we've needed to express our true feelings toward one other. It's given us some techniques to express our (not right or wrong) feelings to each other. After all the hurt we have felt and all the terrible things we have said and done to each other, I really needed to hear that you still love me and that you forgive me for not being perfect.

I pray to God that you and I both realize how much we love each other and how empty our lives would be without each other. This weekend, I have been able to affirm my love, my unconditional love, for you. I think marriages are made in heaven, and I got an angel. I truly got a red-headed angel, so beautiful, strong, wise, gentle, and soft. They definitely broke the mold when they made you. Thanks for loving me and focusing on the truly important things in life with me. Thank you for expressing yourself to me, even when it hurt. I am thankful for so many things in life, and that is why I want to go on living. Basically, I have lots of unfinished business with God, you, Nicole, Renee, Tyler, and our community for all the above reasons.

I want to dream the impossible dream.

Fight the impossible fight.

Run the impossible race.

Tell you all the things that were once impossible to say.

Love you, Love you.

I'll always commit to you, Julie. You'll always have my heart. I'll always continue to be sorry for what I did. I'll always continue to think of you, love you, and show you. I'll continue to provide for you and to help make your life secure and safe. I'll continue to love you, play with you, and enjoy with you. I'll continue to talk with you, express my feelings with you, and love you. I'll continue to disagree with you when I disagree with you. I'll continue to be faithful to you, knowing that you will always be faithful to me. I'll continue not to sin against God and you. I'll continue to work on us. I'll not take you for granted. I'll love you! I'll dialogue with you. I'll feed you when you are hungry. I'll make you smile when you are sad. I'll shelter you when you are out in the cold. I'll hold you when you are feeling insecure. I'll Love You, I'll Love You.

With all my life and love,

Lee

It was a bit excessive, dramatic, repetitive, and at times, ridiculous and funny; the exact words I would use to describe Lee as a person. My anger antennas went up upon reading the line, "You are a great person, not perfect. I am a great person, not perfect either," because it indicated sameness between us, and although I could not agree with that, I tucked the antennas back in and appreciated the other kind, heartfelt sentiments. I was in a good mood when I wrote him back:

To my dearest Lee,

I think you are incredible. You have risked everything in order to be everything to me. I want to go on living because of you, because of the kids, and because I believe God has a purpose for me—but I honestly believe that purpose includes you. I truly believe that in order to fulfill God's purpose, we must be together. We are going to do great things—we are already doing great things. Together we will serve God, and the plan He has for us will become more apparent as the years go by.

When we first met, I adored your smile and easy laughter. What a heart-melting smile you have! As we got to know one another better, I fell in love with your optimism and fun-loving attitude. I loved the fact that you didn't try to kiss me good night after our first evening walk. I loved the fact that you kept driving off the road, because you couldn't stop looking at me on the way to Pancake Days. I loved that you wanted to take me to Pancake Days—I love going places with you—road tripping. It's one of the things I look forward to the most in the whole world—getting away and spending time with you.

At college, I loved the fact that everybody knew you, and everybody liked you. I was glad that you were close to your family, but also, I was jealous. I wanted you all to myself. I still want you just as badly or more now than I did when we first fell in love. Even though it may seem as if I am pushing you away from me as hard as I possibly can, I am only pushing with one arm. The other arm has a tight grip holding on to you for dear life, and inside my head and my heart, I'm praying that you won't go away. I long for nothing more than to be near you!

Your optimistic, fun-loving ways make you special to me, but your newfound love for God and desire to be Christlike makes you extra special to me now. And I think we need each other to continue on our journey to be Christians. We can help one another tremendously in the days, weeks, and years to come. Yes—years! I love thinking about our years to come. The pain of the past will lessen, and we will experience love as few others can. We will experience the love of total acceptance. Because I am able to accept you just the way you are. You are human. You have made mistakes. But you are, also, somebody with a lot of love to give—and I am somebody too. There's a pair of us. Don't tell. They'd banish us, you know. Most people don't experience love to this extent. Let's not let go.

When I punish you for the past, I am not accepting myself for who I am—a person who also makes mistakes and feels great remorse about them. When I condemn you, I am also condemning myself and keeping myself from being the Christlike person I so desire to be. Please remember this and continue to love me even as I berate and belittle you, and please find it in your heart to continue to forgive me. It is I who is the sinner and breaker of the Ten Commandments. I need your love and support always, always, always.

I cherish our love and believe it can and does impact everyone around us—and I believe we can use it to impact an infinite number of people. That is my dream. I want it to be our dream. I want to model for the whole world the love of God and true love between a man and a woman. I am yours, and I love you!!

Forever, Forever,
Miss Juliene

I surprised myself with that letter; particularly since others I had written that weekend weren't as hopeful. It still surprises me every time I read it. Like Lee's letter, it was a bit excessive and dramatic, but I believe God was with us as we wrote, and He can be excessive and dramatic Himself. Just look at how He used His Son to save the world. He allowed him to be nailed by his hands and feet to a cross until he died. Now that's drama!

The weekend concluded with a mass and a renewal of marriage vows. I truly wanted to make those vows with the intention of totally investing in the marriage and moving on from the past, but I knew it was too soon. I took them sincerely with the intention of continuing to try moving forward. And for the first time, I believe that Lee made them sincerely too.

Just before we left the hotel we were approached about becoming a team couple and leading future retreats. Before D-day I would have been thrilled, but now we were too broken to help others. It would be like asking Bill and Hillary to give marital advice, and that seemed ludicrous. Still Lee and I *dialogued* about it when we got home. We wrote down our feelings about it separately, and the fact that he completed his while in front of the television confirmed for me that it wasn't right for us. I wrote:

Dear Lee,

I am feeling a little upset that you are *dialoguing* in front of the television. Can't you give your full attention to me and the topic? I feel sad right now. I'm thinking we shouldn't be a lead couple. We roller coaster too much, and as usual, I want more than I can have. We don't deal well with the influences on our relationship from the outside world. As long as we are allowed to spend forty-eight hours together, not dealing with anything but us, we're great. But when kids, work, television, school, etc, are thrown back in, I think we struggle—too much to be a team couple.

I'm sad,
Julie

I suppose I was being overly sensitive, because his letter, written from the couch, surprised me.

Dear Juliene,

I really felt proud that we were picked to be a team couple. It somehow helped verify my belief that we are destined to be together. I think it would be a great experience, challenging, and very helpful. I'm not sure if I could even get through my love letters to you. I know it would take some time. I think we could help many couples with what we've been through, where we are at, and where we are headed. Weekends away sound great to me. We need to find out more about the time commitment. Is there any training offered? My gut feeling is, I think I would like to try it. But I'm a little nervous about crying so much that I couldn't get through it. I'm sure I would get better. I need to pray on it some more. It was a lot of work and mentally draining. We were both pretty exhausted.

But it was also one of the best weekends of my life. I think it could really help us. I think we would be very good at it. I'm really excited about finding out more about it. At the same time, I hate to commit more of our time away from our family. But if I truly want to serve God, I think this is a good way to do it. I'm definitely very open to the idea. I really enjoy doing things with you. If your heart is against it, I don't have a problem not doing it. On the other hand, if you feel comfortable talking about us, so do I; however, I still feel for what I did. I'm not sure if I want everyone to know about it. I guess we could talk about our level of comfort. In a lot of words, my initial love letter answer is: yes, I would be interested in looking into it. I would like to *dialogue* more on it. I'll tell you one thing; I'm really going to enjoy *dialoguing* with you. Yours forever, Lee

When we exchanged letters, I felt badly, like a mother who criticizes the way a child has drawn a beautiful picture. I became acutely aware that, over the years, I had been overly critical in regard to insignificant matters. The infidelities deserved judgment. *But should judgment be passed on where he sits when he writes me a letter, how he loads the dishwasher, the color he paints the swing set, the direction he mows the grass, the way he leaves the toilet, or how he folds a towel?*

The Marriage Encounter Weekend taught that there are three stages of love: romance, disillusionment, and at last, the joy that comes from making the decision to love. I was still in stage two, and true joy was alluding me; however, I was climbing Mt. Joy one step at a time with the assistance of God's messages and His messengers. The lead couples at the marriage seminar were examples of the joy that can come when a couple decides to continue loving after the disillusionment. Lee was also pushing me along with his continued commitment to change. I would keep climbing.

CHAPTER

Forty-Nine

While I was attending graduate school, taking care of our home and children, and rebuilding my marriage, I was also working part-time as the confirmation coordinator for our church. The job was a God thing in a couple of ways. First of all, it encouraged me to do the work of loving more and judging less. Hypocrisy was my enemy, so teaching young people to be more Christlike while punishing my husband day after day felt like feeding my enemy and making him stronger, so I worked to listen to my own words in order to starve the enemy and feed my desire to do what Jesus would do. Next, the job led me to friendships with women, Christian women. One Christian woman whom I'll call Trixie was a youth minister whose desk faced mine in a cramped office where we laughed and laughed and then laughed some more. We laughed at ourselves, our husbands, the world, and we laughed at the fact that we were laughing so much.

And we were honest with one another. She told me I was great with the youth, and I told her she was better. When I sang " Top of the World" and danced around the office, she told me that she hated The Carpenters and that she wasn't fond of my singing either. And when her constant sniffling drove me up a wall, I gave her a box of Kleenex. We could be sardonic and brutally honest one minute and praise the Lord and one another the next. I had never experienced a friendship so uplifting and real before. She was a blessing to me at a time when I could use an extra one.

Trixie and I, plus another coworker, a nun, and a few ladies from the church formed the Trust Group. We met one night a month to share dinner and our struggles. In a circle of friendship, lit by candles and supported by acceptance, I opened up about my husband's unfaithfulness, while others processed childhood abuse, challenging offspring, and everyday stress. Sometimes, free of judgment and full of faith, we cried, and sometimes we laughed so hard that we cried. At the end of the evening, we would link hands and send out prayers for one another to a gracious and wonderful God who had to be thrilled that we were together and demonstrating His love toward each other.

Trixie gave each of us prayer journals, and I used that book to write letters to God about my continued inner conflict between being a Christian forgiver and being a resentful, scorned woman. On February 28, 1997, I wrote:

Dear Lord,

As the one year anniversary of finding out the *awful* truth approaches, I begin to feel awful, because I'm not keeping my word. I'm not pushing the thoughts away. Instead I'm dwelling on them. Why am I choosing to make myself miserable? Why do I desire to relive every *awful* moment of a year ago? I've got to pull myself up again, because I can feel the sadness beginning to engulf me. Lord—please forgive me my self-centeredness. Forgive me for thinking my cross is too heavy. Help me to allow you to carry my cross for me. And help me to fully live my days today and not waste them on the past.

Amen

I would occasionally write letters of thankfulness and words of contentment in that prayer journal, but most often I was asking for forgiveness, because I couldn't forgive. Trixie and the other ladies challenged me to be better, and with their encouragement I could sometimes decide to love my husband more fully and without inhibition.

CHAPTER

Fifty

A few days before the one-year anniversary of the death of our old marriage, Lee was notified that he was being transferred to Iowa. In my journal, I wrote of feeling "great anxiety" and "a wild fear." The move would take us closer to our families, but further from the support system of women that I had been able to create for myself, as well as take me away from the job I loved and my schooling. The move could be a new beginning for Lee and me, or it could be the beginning of another ending. The year since finding out had often been horrendous, but it had also been empowering. And although I had lost my faith in Lee, I had gained an infinitely deeper trust in God, the truth that I was not a victim but a survivor, and faith that God would never leave me. I had frequently asked God to lead our lives, and therefore, I believed the move was God-driven, but I was extremely concerned about the few months we would be living apart. Lee would begin his new job in April, and the kids and I would follow him in June once we finished the school year. He would be alone in a new town, and I was absolutely certain temptation resided there.

During the past six months, Lee started to drink again. He would have a single glass of wine with dinner or a cocktail or two when we were out with friends. I wanted him to be able to drink in moderation when we were being social, and I enjoyed sharing a glass of wine with him over dinner. I didn't want him drinking to excess and drinking when I wasn't around. Considering the circumstances, I thought my expectations were fairly reasonable. But how would that work when three hundred miles separated us?

Speaking of drinking, something odd had happened. He was no longer able to drink beer without becoming sick. His eyes would get very red, and he would get a full feeling and sometimes throw up. He swore I had put some kind of a spell on him that caused this intolerance. I suppose one night I may have arisen from my bed, my red hair matted and frizzy, and my black robe dragging the floor, and floated into the kitchen. It's possible I could have placed a pan on the stove and tossed in some rose petals, water, and honey, and as they rose to a boil, I might have chanted the following in my very best witch voice:

No more drink,
Beer is bad.
When you drink it,
My soul is sad.
Burden you become,
Wench I am one.
So drink no more,
Sleep with no more whore.
Kind is your life,
Love only for your wife.
Love me more than you love you,
And never again drink the brew!

At that point I might have poured in some beer along with a lock of Lee's hair and thrown back my head and laughed an eerie laugh. I suppose I might have done that, but I don't think so.

So he couldn't drink beer anymore, and when offered one, he enjoyed saying, "I can't drink it. Julie put a hex on me, and now I'm allergic to it." Then he liked to use a line that I'd made up for him, "If I drink it, I break out into an idiot." I'm not sure why I didn't include hard liquor in my magic spell, but thus far, he always stopped at two. The post-separation drink protocol called for no more than two drinks in an evening and no more than one an hour. He assured me that after he moved he would not go to bars and he would call me every night before he went to sleep. He reminded me that he was a different man and all he wanted was me and the kids, and our family. I believed him, but the past still terrified me. How could I know that he wouldn't get wasted and feel lonely and seek out some inviting female like he had in the past?

I couldn't know. The hard and well-known truth was there were no guarantees. I had made the decision to stay in the marriage, and I could do no more than set up parameters and hope (and pray), he would be willing to stay within them in order to help me feel more secure. For 95 percent of the last year, that strategy had worked out well; however, 5 percent of the time, I sensed the vibrations of his self-centeredness tank rolling back into town. At times he lost patience with my distrust. At times, if I expressed my fears, he defended his right to drink, and at times his newfound gentleness in the bedroom was replaced with disrespect. These issues were disturbing, but we were learning to work through them more quickly, i.e., within a day, he took full responsibility for what he might have done to upset me.

Once he left for Iowa, I was so busy finishing my graduate course work, keeping the house, which was on the market, clean, taking care of the kids, and preparing for the move that I had no time to worry about the choices that my husband might be making. I gave it up to God: *Lord, I don't have time or energy to fret about whether Lee is choosing to get drunk and sleep with someone else. You watch over and guide him, please. Thank You.*

CHAPTER

Fifty-One

A man named Carl Bard once said, "Though no one can go back and make a new start, anyone can start from now and make a brand new end." That quote sparked my *can do* attitude and became my mantra as we began life back in the Hawkeye State. When the kids and I joined Lee during the summer of '97, we lived in a two-bedroom apartment while our new home was being built. Most of our furniture was put into storage, and we lived for four months as if we were camping. The kids shared a queen-size mattress that had no bed frame. Our living room furniture consisted of four foldout chairs. We watched a thirteen-inch television, and we ate out most of the time. The complex had a pool, and when we weren't swimming, we were exploring the book shops, consignment stores, and the malls of our new town. It was fun, and it was easy, and I was happy that we were still a family, embarking on a new adventure together.

I had heard it said that building a home could easily end a marriage, but our tastes were similar, and Lee deferred to me most of the time, so it went smoothly. Once we were in the new house in late October and the kids had gotten used to their new home and school, the first year flew by. We passed the two-year anniversary of that no good, really bad day without a hitch, and when our thirteenth wedding anniversary was approaching in the fall of '98, Lee planned a trip for him and me to fly to Lake Tahoe and stay at a bed and breakfast.

Lee more readily invested in trips for us now, and when he complained about the money, I would, half in jest, ask him how much he thought a divorce would cost. Quality time together made me happy; somehow choosing happiness came more easily from a beautiful tourist location. He too would become giddy about our trips, especially when he planned them. This one was no different. Because of his inability to keep secrets—happy ones that is—he kept hinting that everything was going to be extra special, starting with the rental car.

"You're going to like it," he told me, grinning, when we were still thirty thousand feet in the air. "I'm sure I will," I told him, not overcome with anticipation, since he was known for reaching *I won the lottery* excitement levels when he found a couple dollars in his jean's pocket. I knew better than to hope that a luxury vehicle would be tooling us around the lake.

However, we were both surprised a couple of hours later when the number given to us by the Avis agent matched us up to a red, two-door, extended cab, Ford Ranger mini truck.

"I thought that, when I asked for a four-wheel drive, I was going to get a jeep or an SUV. I wasn't expecting a little, red truck!" Lee exclaimed.

"It's fine," I assured him, giggling. "Really, it's fine. It'll be fun. We'll be stylin' in Ralph the Red Ranger, and if there's a snowstorm in October, we'll be prepared."

The drive would have been spectacular in any vehicle as long as it had windows, because Lake Tahoe was the bluest, most gorgeous lake I had ever seen. I was so awed by the size and the sheer beauty of it that I found myself wishing I were Jesus and could walk across it, gazing down into the crystal clear water at all the creatures living below.

"Beautiful!" I heard Lee say. "And I don't mean the lake, Jewel. I mean you."

We pulled into the B&B a little while later. Like Bonny Brooke Farms in Arkansas, this bed and breakfast had cabins separated from the main lodge. It was located on the peaceful, West Shore of the lake, and the charming, red cottages were surrounded by huge pine trees. We unpacked in a quaint little getaway house that was complete with fireplace and claw foot tub, and then we went to the main house to inquire about a nearby restaurant and spent a few minutes munching on brie and crackers while becoming acquainted with our hosts before jumping back in Ralph to go to dinner.

I don't recall what we had to eat or even where we went, but I remember we shared the meal. Meal sharing had become a habit over the previous couple of years. It was a way to save money, but more importantly, it allowed us to be less full at the end of dinner, so we usually had room for dessert. That night and every meal following, we ate exactly the same thing. And we also took vitamins. These weren't just any old vitamins; they were supposed to build endurance and stamina. We had gotten them in a goody bag passed out at a race we had run in, and we thought, *What better time to try out an energy supplement than during our vacation together?* We wanted to have endurance. Lee wanted to have stamina.

By the middle of the second day our digestive systems had been working on the various food items and vitamin supply. It first happened in Ralph the Red Ranger as were driving around the lake looking for the ideal picnic location. Suddenly, and without any sort of warning, it was there, and it was horrendous.

"Oh my Lord!" I yelled. "What is that God-awful smell?"

I looked at Lee, and his face was filled with shame like a child who has just pooped his pants. "What have you done?" I questioned.

"I'm so sorry," he said, "I think I have a little gas."

"Oh *my gosh*! Nothing about that was little. I think you crapped yourself." I hurriedly rolled down the window and stuck my head out and gulped in the fresh air. I truly had never smelled anything so atrocious.

"It just kind of snuck up on me," he said with embarrassment.

"Well, I don't know about that, but next time, give a girl some warning, would you?"

A while later he did give warning as we sat on a large rock next to the lake, enjoying strawberries and wine. He tried to step away, but he could not move quickly enough on the jagged and uneven rocks at the water's edge.

"Oh, honey! That really puts a damper on the picnic," I said as I scrunched up my face and then buried my nose in my hands.

"I know, sweetie. I'm sorry, but I think something crawled up inside me and died. I can't understand it, because you and I have been eating all the same food."

"A smell that bad could never come out of me," I said.

Well, that was a lie. My digestive system must have been working more slowly than his, and it caught up to me on the ride back to the bed and breakfast. When I felt it coming on, there was no way of stopping it. I sat silently and when the smell flooded the cab of the truck, I did what any good Christian girl would do, I yelled, "What the heck? Are you kidding me? You were supposed to give me some warning."

He turned to look at me and his nose hit the now familiar scent, and he said, "Oh, honey. I didn't notice that one coming on. I'm so sorry. I didn't even realize I did it."

I giggled a little but gave nothing away as my face registered disgust once again. Through the now open window, I began to breathe as the stale air evaporated. Yes, I felt some guilt but not enough to fess up. It was just too funny and endearing that he took the blame and didn't consider it might have been me.

He assumed blame again back in the room when my funk saturated the air of our cabin. He was shocked at how the gas was escaping him without him being aware, and he was incredibly apologetic.

"Jewel," he said. "You don't even know how sorry I am, and I would like to give you warning, but I'm just not getting any myself. I truly don't even know I'm doing it."

I laughed harder this time, but he thought I was finding humor in the situation as he knew it. The fact that it didn't occur to him that it could be me exuding that amazingly bad smell was amazing. I continued to snicker quietly to myself but betrayed nothing until we were shopping some time later that day. We had gone into a men's store at an outdoor mall, and Lee had found a couple of pair of pants that he wanted to try on, and since the dressing room was rather large and had a chair in it, he invited me to sit in while he changed. I felt it coming on again, and as he was unbuckling his belt, the gas escaped me. When he dropped his jeans to the floor, the smell permeated that dressing area and hit us both at the same time. We looked at one another in horror.

"Jiminy crap!" he said. "I swear I didn't see that coming, Jewel. I think it's stuck in my pants, and I need to go back to the room and shower and change clothes. I'm so, so sorry!"

That was too much for me. I fell to the ground in hysterics, tears rolling from my eyes as I laughed and laughed on that dressing room floor. The room had a partial door that was open at least a foot from the floor, so anyone looking under to see if the room was in use would have seen me lying there laughing uproariously. My husband had never been more sweet or funnier to me, and even my riot on the floor did not clue him in to what was really going on.

"Jewel, I swear I don't even know it's happening," he said. "I'm so glad you can laugh about it, because I just feel terrible."

That made me laugh even harder, and then I started pointing to myself and mouthing that it was me who was passing the gas. It took him a second to register what I was trying to tell him, and then his eyes got wide as he asked, "You did it?"

I nodded my head and continued laughing.

"You piece of crap!" he said. "All day long I've been taking the blame for your stinky ass farts? Are you serious?!"

I pushed myself to sit up against the wall and attempted to get it together as I continued nodding my head.

"I can't believe it," he said.

"It's true," I replied, wiping away tears. "I'm sorry, but it was just so darn funny that you kept thinking it was you. You're hilarious."

"You're something else," he said.

By the time he had made his decision, I had pulled myself together. As we left the store, I linked my arm with his and asked, "Are we still friends?"

"You're in trouble, and you're going to have to be punished," he responded with a coy smile.

The next day we went to the grocery store, and I found him in the periodicals section, staring at the cover of a *Maxim Magazine*, which featured a perfectly gorgeous woman, scantily clad, who oozed sex out of her every pore. My gas-passing, fun-loving, lighthearted attitude instantly evaporated as I realized that the old Lee would never completely disappear.

CHAPTER
Fifty-Two

As Lee's old behaviors began creeping back into our lives, I felt them light a fire under my pot of residual anxiety and anger. It was not only that he had ogled a flawless model on the cover of a magazine, but he was drinking more frequently and more heavily. In fact, he had gone for drinks after work one night and had come home drunk at two in the morning, which had lead to a huge argument.

Three years after finding out about the infidelities, I still could not make peace with his unfaithfulness, mostly because of his recent backslide into uncomfortable territory. Continuing to contemplate what my life would be like if we ended our marriage, I came to the conclusion that if we divorced, he would need to find a woman with a vagina in order to be happy while I would need to find a man with a brain. His chances for happiness post-divorce appeared to be significantly greater than mine.

I realize I had become cynical. I didn't like that about myself, and I also didn't like who Lee was becoming again, so we headed back to counseling, which turned out to be a successful move, because we were both laughing by the time we reached our car after the first session. The counselor, who appeared to be 110 and could no longer see or hear, had held his notepad two inches from his face and scribbled notes or possibly drew pictures throughout the session. No matter what we said, he would nod his head and say, "I see," which was a lie. We could have commented on aliens forcing us to salsa dance with one another all night long, and he would have kept nodding. With or without that counselor's help, somehow we continued to hang tightly to our marriage pendulum that swung between the extremes of unhappiness and unbridled joy.

CHAPTER

Fifty-Three

When the pendulum was swinging toward happiness, we tended to make uncharacteristic decisions, which climaxed toward the end of 2002, when we found ourselves confronted by a dog dilemma. Lee and I had agreed early in the marriage that neither of us ever wanted to have a dog that stayed in the house, so when we saw that cute, little, yellow, Labrador retriever puppy with the big brown eyes, we told Tyler, who was now nine, "No, absolutely not." We already had a German shorthaired hunting dog, named Maggie, which stayed outside in a kennel, and we struggled to find time to take her for walks and plan for her when we needed to be away, so it did not make sense to get another dog that could potentially end up inside the house increasing my already overwhelming housework.

"But Mom, he's so cute," responded my son as he bent down to snuggle the blonde, furry creature under his chin.

He was indeed cute. I didn't want to admit it to Ty, but this was the kind of puppy that caused me to grit my teeth, wring my hands, and ache to hold him like a newborn baby. I wanted to cuddle that puppy until his body grew to match his paw size, but once he was full grown, cuddling would include a lot of shedding and an excessive amount of drool.

"He's kind of cute," I admitted, fighting back my urge to snatch that mini pile of adorableness up in my arms and nuzzle my nose into his warm fur. "But you know your dad and I don't want a dog in the house, and we already have Maggie."

"Maggie needs company," my son argued. "Once this puppy grows up, he can stay outside with Maggie, and they can be friends."

His argument was logical, and not only was the puppy precious, but Tyler holding the puppy was off-the-charts cute. Despite my better judgment, I wanted my son to have this puppy; however, we didn't even know if having this puppy as our own was an option. We had arrived at my in-laws' farm only moments before, and since the puppy was chained in their front yard, it seemed likely that he was my father-in-law's latest pet, *Which would*, I thought, *solve the problem.*

However, Grandpa offered to sell us Petey, the name he had already given him, for the bargain price of $25, the going rate for a full-blooded lab in the Southeastern Iowa town of Fort Madison. He would then use the money to buy another puppy from the litter. Tyler went back and forth between his dad and me: "Can I have him, please? It's only twenty-five dollars. Please?"

We gave in more easily than I would have ever expected, but the cuteness factor skewed our thinking. The puppy sat on Tyler's lap on the way home, and his sisters were as excited as he was to have their friends see their newest younger brother. Only about fifteen minutes had passed before we began to understand the complications that accompanied our addition to the family.

"Mom, Petey's wetting on me," squealed my son.

"Ewww!" cried the girls as they pushed themselves to the furthest edges of the seat.

"Put him on the floor," I suggested too late.

That would be the first of several accidents and messes that the Petey Man would make. But like a young child that is easily forgiven for not knowing better, so was Petezzeria, the dog of many names, granted absolution, at least by me and the kids. We thought it was hilarious when we asked, "Petester, what did you do?" and he responded by leaning his head way back to avoid making eye contact. Lee, on the other hand, didn't think it was so funny, and he was slower to forgive an episode of uncontrolled bladder, shredded sock, or the regurgitation of a pop bottle lid.

On an evening when we were all watching a movie together, Needy Petey, the attention-seeker, kept dropping his ball in front of each of us as we tried to concentrate on the television screen, taking turns absentmindedly at throwing the ball into the open kitchen area for him to retrieve. Unintentionally, I had thrown the ball under the desk that had a ladder-back chair pulled into it. Unaware of how much he had grown, Peter Pan stuck his head under the chair to retrieve his toy. As he tried to back out with his ball in his mouth, his shoulders caught on the rung of the chair and, panicking, he jerked his head up and threw the chair into the air, in the process capturing our full attention.

But that was not all. When Nicole cried, "Aw! What's that smell?" we noticed that Poor Pete had had an accident.

With Lee's help, it got cleaned up, but when the rest of us tried to console Petey by chanting, "If you love Petey and you know it, clap your hands," I noticed that Lee was reluctant to do any such thing. And I took it to heart.

Even though several years had passed since the day of revelations, I still had meltdowns. If a show or a song or a bad decision, on Lee's part, pulled the memory to the forefront of my mind, and I was not strong enough to push it away, I would cry. I would lie on the couch while everyone was gone, and I would relive my hurt once again while Sweetie Petey sat like a rock of strength beside me. He would rest his head on my lap or beside me on the couch, and he would gaze at me with love and acceptance. He just let me sob without judgment and never left my side.

CHAPTER

Fifty-Four

"The struggle continues," I wrote in my journal in the spring of 2004. "The Goddamn struggle continues." Then I apologized to God for taking His name in vain, and I told Him it would be easier for me to keep His commandments if other people did as well. That's not to say that Lee had *coveted* the neighbor's wife again, but he did go jogging with her.

It started out being a small group of people running together, myself included. Over time, people dropped out, and since I was slower than those who remained, I was often treated to a view featuring my husband's backside and that of a beautiful, intelligent, athletic friend. I tried not to make a big deal out of the fact that they left me behind, because I didn't want to slow them down; however, I was hurt and jealous of her speed and her fake breasts. I tried, subtly, to convey the fact that the situation bothered me to Lee, but, in his mind, it was all about the workout.

One morning he said he was going to lift weights at the club instead of running, so I stayed home. As I lay in bed, I regretted not going with him, because I was unable to fall back asleep, so I hopped up and decided to join him. When I entered the club, the woman at the counter said, "If you were planning to run with Lee and Anne, they've already left."

I hesitated for a second before saying, "No, I'm not running today." I got on the treadmill and intended to walk a couple of miles, but I was too upset. I got off the treadmill, walked myself right past the check-in girl, and went back home where I sat down at the computer and wrote about my continuing struggle with distrust.

By the time Lee returned home about an hour later, I was shaking all over, a symptom I had come to recognize as a sign of post-traumatic stress disorder, which manifested itself whenever the present resembled the past. I could never completely forget the past, but he could. He could forgive himself and lie to me about running. I hated him for that, yet I didn't hate him. I loved him, and I loved us. There were so many intimate moments now, like the Sunday when we had wrestled in bed, and I had told him that this was not a day of breast but a day of rest. Such moments were my happiest, and I didn't want to give them up, but I hated the fear. I refused to stay a casualty of the past and his unfaithfulness, but in these moments, I felt so vulnerable.

I turned away from the computer to face him as he walked by the den. When he saw me, he said, grinning, "Hey, you're supposed to be waiting in bed for me."

"I decided that if you want to lie to me and run with Anne," I told him, grimly, "you can go screw yourself."

"Julie, I ran to warm up before weights," he said calmly. "And I can't be honest with you, because you get all bent out of shape like you are right now."

"You're darn right I get bent out of shape," I retorted. "After all that we've been through, I can't believe you would expect otherwise. And you're a jerk!" I threw in for good measure. "If you'd just wanted a short, little, warm-up run, you would have invited me to come with you. But you didn't want me to infringe on your plans to run with her."

"You are invited to run with us every morning," he said, disappearing into the kitchen.

"Yeah, so I can run behind and watch your asses take off ahead of me?"

Making no response, he set about making his usual breakfast. I wanted him to feel sick to his stomach like I did. But he didn't. And when he was about to leave for work, he simply said, "I just wanted to get in a workout. Sex was not on my mind."

"Obviously, since you chose to leave my bed."

I was mad at myself after that, because that was not a very good comeback, and then he was gone. I struggled to choose happiness in times like these, because I allowed my dysfunctional relationship to cloud my view of the world, and I lost my perspective.

But I did hear God say, "Others in this world are suffering much more than you are."

❧

Lee called me. That is why I get sucked in again. He tries to fix things. I didn't allow him to fix them immediately, but he called. Then he called again later that day. He told me he would only run with me from now on, and he was sorry for being so selfish. He said that I was the only woman he would ever want. I maintained the cold tone of my voice, but I was thawing rapidly, until the next fight.

Lee had to go to Chicago on business. Our agreement was that he would call me every night before he went to bed so I could hear his voice and be reassured. On this particular trip, he didn't call the last night. I tried to call him, but he didn't answer, and the last time I tried, it went straight to voicemail, so I went on to bed feeling crappy once again. I tossed and turned, and at two in the morning, wrote the following poem:

> Is up, up? Or down, down?
> If I said right was left or left was right, would it then be so?
> Do I think life is good, because it is?
> Or do I think life is good; therefore, it is?
> Is my life really a pile of crap?
> If crap thinks it is a filet, does that make it so?
> No, but the crap feels better thinking that way.
> My life is crap that keeps trying to will itself into being a filet.

I then slept until almost six, at which time, realizing that he had never called, I was jolted into a state of extreme anxiety. And then, since his cell phone was still going to voice mail, I called his room, and when he answered, demanded to know why he hadn't called. And when he said that, by the time he could, it was too late and that he hadn't wanted to wake me, I said, "I don't care, but I do care if you have been out sleeping around on me. Did you get drunk and sleep with someone?"

He laughed when I said that and when I asked him what was so funny, he said, "I love you."

I cussed him then, but not out loud, because I was trying to be better. I thought he was a narcissistic pig, and I hated him, but really I didn't, and there was the problem all over again.

I told him I had to go, because it was long distance and costing money. He apologized again and said he loved me, but he didn't insist that we stay on the phone until I felt better. He didn't say, "I'll call you back." We hung up, and I swore some more in my head, and I loathed him and his despicable idiocy. I thought about him being an idiot and not being able to see beyond himself, and I ranted and raved, and then I recalled that I had gone to confession on the previous evening. Was the devil getting me so worked up?

Was I supposed to be better? Was I never supposed to get angry? Was that what God asked of me?

I didn't know, so I continued feeling hatred. Hatred for all the horrible things my husband had ever done and frustration toward all the people who had ever let me down. *Was I the only person on the planet who wanted to do right? Ha, I was definitely letting the devil in. Only he could give me such an ego.*

When Lee arrived home later that day, the entire world was in trouble, but only he and seventeen-year-old Renee, whom I had recently caught inappropriately messaging her boyfriend, were on hand to provide an outlet for my wrath. By the time we went to bed that night, none of us was on speaking terms. Nicole had left a few weeks earlier for college, and Tyler had moved his room to the basement, so the next morning, with Lee and me dodging one another in our bathroom and Renee fixing her hair in hers, I couldn't take it anymore. Going to the top of the stairs between the two bathrooms, looking like a fool with my wet, disheveled hair and no makeup, wearing only a bathrobe, I shouted, "I can't be everyone's moral meter anymore! Telling you to do this or don't do that. Saying this is wrong, but that is right."

Both of them had come out to stare at me.

"It's hard enough to make the right choices for myself every day," I gasped. "I can't do this anymore. If you want to act out, make bad choices, whatever, I can't stop you. You're both grown and can do whatever the hell you want."

Lee was looking at me as though I was being ridiculous, and so I stumbled down the stairs and into the den, where I put my head in my hands and sobbed. I was so tired of fighting people, mainly Lee, to get them to make positive choices, healthy choices. Why did it have to be so hard?

Lee followed me and said he was sorry. He said he was not out to hurt me; he just had too much to drink, and went on to say, "Most people wouldn't even apologize."

I had the urge to scream at the top of my lungs for the rest of my life, but instead I reminded him that most people don't forgive what I had worked to forgive. Or did they? Who even knew? Maybe I was trying to make myself a martyr when many people forgive infidelity and I just didn't know about it. I was torn between feeling like a saint for forgiving and feeling like a nag for still reminding him of what he'd done. If I was still bringing it up, didn't that mean I really hadn't forgiven? I certainly hadn't forgotten, but it sure seemed as if he had. In order to heal completely, I needed to forget and he needed to remember.

CHAPTER

Fifty-Five

Lee and I celebrated our twentieth wedding anniversary in Hawaii. I thought that meant he remembered. During the long flight over the Pacific Ocean, we reminisced without bringing up the elephant in the room. To be honest, I didn't want nor need it to be brought up, because I was happy. I was able to think of the infidelity like a badge of honor, because we had fought through that war and appeared to have come out victorious. We were still together, we were still a family, and we were still laughing. At one point on the flight I had leaned into him, looked him in the eyes, and said, "I can't wait to make love to you later," and when he replied, "What makes you think I'm a sure thing?" we both collapsed laughing.

When I wasn't being entertained by his witty comebacks, we were both amused by the letters that had been given to us in a gift bag before we left. We had been instructed not to open it until we were in the air, so not long after takeoff, we pulled out the tissue paper on top and found eight envelopes labeled with messages, such as "We love you a lot," and "You're wonderful," written with a colored marker. Inside each envelope was a letter written by one of the following: Nicole; her boyfriend, Kyle; Renee; her boyfriend, Mark; Tyler; Nicole's best friend, Kelsey; and Renee's best friends, Kate and Sara. Each of them had wished us well and expressed appreciation for things we had done for them over the years.

Lee and I had tears in our eyes as we read messages from their friends, such as, "I admire the two of you because of the examples that you set and how you treat each other and the people around you," "You are by far the most fun couple that I know," "You guys are awesome parents, not only to your kids but to others," and also, "Your family and its closeness is something I truly admire."

The children added touches of humor with such gems as, "I hope you have tons of fun on your trip, even though I don't really see how you can without me being there with you," "You may not have known much about parenting in the beginning, but along the way you have developed into what I believe to be the *perfect* parents," and, "If you have been making out on the plane, you should probably stop, because I assume the people next to you are probably feeling pretty uncomfortable right now."

The letters were the perfect anniversary gifts from our children, and when we stepped off the plane, the weather and beautiful scenery of Maui were the perfect gift from God. I felt rewarded in many ways for staying in the marriage. Once we were in the rental car and on our way to the resort, I reached over to hold Lee's hand.

Throughout our stay we took advantage of various activities that were offered, both on the island and at the resort. We spent an entire day in the car on the Road to Hana. We went to a luau and a *Cirque De Soleil* show. We made love on our private deck, and we went to a water aerobics class taught by a Polynesian man named Kapula. Kapula brought with him a number of swimming noodles to assist us in our workout and would encourage us to "reach aaallllll the way down your noodle," which cracked us up. Lee thought it would be even funnier to tell Kapula that I kept trying to grab his noodle.

"If you do," I told Lee," I'll tell him that I'm not touching anything of yours. Now keep that thing away from me and pay attention."

It was wonderful to be away together, enjoying ourselves.

At first, we truly had fun on that tropical island in the North Pacific.

And then we didn't anymore.

∽

The night before we left for home, the bar at the resort offered free happy hour drinks. The words *free* and *happy hour* should never be used together. In fact, the word *free* should never be used around Lee, period. Numerous objects were lying around our house, which were of no use, but they were *free*. We had a sink lying on the ground in the garage, tires that took up space in the shed, and boxes of old newspapers stacked in our storage space in the basement. We had also attended presentations on timeshares and job opportunities in order to get *free* stuff. So the words *free happy hour* brought us two different reactions. I wanted to take off running straight into the ocean to avoid the train wreck that I saw coming, and he wanted to run as fast as his legs would take him to the front of the free drink line, where he grabbed two drinks, dropped one off for me, and then drank the other while waiting in line for two more.

I didn't run, but I did walk to the beach and sit down on the sand. I looked out over the water and asked that big ocean why my husband was such a fool. I wanted to know what went on in his brain that made him think that getting trashed on free drinks was a good decision on our anniversary, especially considering our past.

Once happy hour was over, he came and found me and asked, "What's wrong with you?"

What was wrong with *me?*

I didn't answer him. I kept scanning the blue waves for answers that unfortunately did not roll in with the ocean tide.

He walked away and left me.

I sat there a while longer and then decided to go in search of the answers. I walked in our room just as he was climbing into bed. It was a little after seven.

"Are you really going to bed?" I asked him. "It's our last night in Hawaii."

"I'm tired."

"You're drunk."

He was quiet, and I was furious. More words were said by me and yelled by me as he nestled himself under the covers and closed his eyes. I slammed the door and left. I wandered the hotel, and then returned to the room to put on my bathing suit. He didn't stir as I moved around and flipped on lights. I was past hoping that he would. Once I was in my suit and cover-up, I went down to the pool and got in the hot tub with strangers. I would have liked to have gone unnoticed as I stepped down into the steaming water, but they were friendly people from Ohio, and they wanted to know where I was from and what was I doing in Hawaii. With pride, I said I was from Iowa, and celebrating my twentieth wedding anniversary. Of course, the question of my spouse's whereabouts came up, so I made an excuse for him, because I certainly didn't want them to feel sorry for me.

I did not want to be viewed as weak because that was not the way I felt. I might have felt tired and worn down by my marriage, but overall I knew I could do all things though Christ who strengthens me. I would be fine. Even though I was soaking in a Jacuzzi tub with strangers on my anniversary, I would be fine.

Lee and I didn't speak on the nine-hour flight home, a flight that seemed more like a week, because I could not rest for fear of accidentally touching him. I was a grade-schooler and he was the kid next to me with cooties. I leaned toward the window as far as I could and tried unsuccessfully to ignore the armrest pressing into my side.

Once back home, I remained cold. He tried to cuddle, and I rejected him. His response to the rejection was to say that he wanted to be with his wife, and if I was going to continue to hold out on him, then he would seek affection elsewhere. And at that moment, that was just fine with me. After all, there was nothing that he could do to me that I had not already lived though.

Days went by, and we hardly spoke. The children, eager not to cause any trouble, were almost invisible. When we went to church and I did not go to communion, they questioned me about it, and I said, "Jesus tells us not to come and receive him if we have anger toward others in our hearts." There was no need for them to ask who I was angry with.

A short while later Lee suggested we attend a Weekend to Remember Marriage Conference that he had heard about on the radio. Smart Lee was back. He knew I would not turn that down. He knew I would see it as an invitation to a party with God.

We were not interacting with one another as we signed in at the conference and found our seats in the large ballroom. My defenses were thick, and even though I had agreed to attend, Lee was not going to break through my walls very easily. God knew that. Introductions were made, prayers were said, and then the presenter made everyone aware that they were being prayed for by someone outside of the conference. Nearly three hundred couples were in attendance, and the speaker read just a few couples' names and stated who was praying for them: "Lee and Julie are being prayed for by Bob in Colorado." I had not expected to hear my name of all the couples in attendance. Knowing that a perfect stranger, living a couple of states away, was praying for us specifically caused all my barriers to come crashing down at once. I slid down in my seat, hoping that no one would notice that I was weeping. Lee put his arm around my shoulders, and I allowed him to hold me. The speaker might as well have said, "Julie, God called, and he wants you to know that he loves you, and he wants you to love your husband."

CHAPTER
Fifty-Six

I love shoes. On one occasion Lee helped me carry nine pairs of shoes out of a Younkers Department Store during their end of summer clearance sale. I also love food and hate to cook, so frequently we would eat out or order in. I love massages, so Lee bought a massage table and regularly would play the role of Sven, my personal masseur. I was spoiled. I never asked for items too outrageous or expensive, and given all that we'd been through, I felt I deserved most anything, so when I asked to have Carlos stay with us, Lee said, "Whatever you want, sweetie," even though I'm certain he would have rather said, "No."

Carlos was a seventeen-year-old foreign exchange student from Sao Paulo, Brazil. A neighbor had pressed us to take on one of the last students that she was trying to place, and I was thrilled at the idea of being an ambassador for our country. The rest of my family were not as enthusiastic when it came to being ministers of goodwill. The girls were attending college so they didn't mind too much, but still Renee was not thrilled about the fact that we would be putting him in her room. As for Tyler, he didn't exactly want to share his parents and his home with a stranger, and Lee was reluctant to be responsible for someone else's child for ten months. But as I said, he indulged me, as usual.

It was August of 2006 when Renee and I went to the airport to meet Carlos for the first time. We had made a big sign that read, "Hola, Carlos! Beinvenido," which was beautifully done, except for the fact, as Carlos, himself, pointed out later, Portuguese was his native language, not Spanish.

And that was just the beginning. The language barrier was a little difficult for all of us to navigate. Lee seemed to believe that the louder he spoke, the more likely it was that Carlos would understand him. On his first day with us, as we drove around town to assist Carlos in becoming acclimated to the area, Lee yelled toward Carlos in the backseat, "Do you have McDonald's in Brazil?"

"He's not deaf," I said. I turned toward Carlos and asked gently, "Carlos, do…you…have…McDonald's…in…Brazil?"

Tyler and Renee rolled their eyes. Renee said, "He's not deaf or a baby. Just talk to him normally. "Do you have McDonald's in Brazil, Carlos?" to which he responded with a yes and a big smile.

He smiled often and was quick to laugh at Lee's jokes. I had been the one to rally for him to stay with us, but it seemed that it was Lee he enjoyed the most. Carlos was amused early Saturday mornings when Lee would holler out, "Game day, baby!" in order to get everyone pumped up for the upcoming Iowa Hawkeye game. On Sundays, Carlos would sometimes watch NFL football with Lee, not because he cared about the games, but more so because he was entertained by Lee's antics. If his fantasy football players did well, he would jump around the room, pumping his arms in the air, and if they didn't do well, he would throw pillows and yell obscenities at the television. Carlos smiled when Lee told him to stop drinking all his Mountain Dew and when he told him to start buying some groceries, and he wasn't offended in the least when he was leaving for a school dance with a date and Lee said, "Keep it in your pants. We don't want any baby Brazilians running around."

Most anything Lee did struck Carlos as funny, so I was a bit bewildered when my jokes were met with blank stares. On the way to a foreign exchange student get-together, Carlos and Tyler were in the backseat, and Carlos was holding the Brazilian hotdogs that he had prepared for the party. When Lee had to suddenly brake in traffic, I shouted, "Boys, hang onto your hotdogs, 'cause Lee's a crazy driver!" I was surprised to find that I was the only one laughing.

Even though I was well aware of the four seasons of our twenty-one-year relationship, which I would characterize as good, really good, great, and a disaster, I might have been hoping that having a guest in our home would mean that we could avoid disaster for a change, but that was, unfortunately, far from being the truth. Instead, the idea had tricked me into a false sense of security and not for the first time.

Lee had lunch with a female coworker. That circumstance should be acceptable and expected in most relationships; however, our relationship was different, and the details around the lunch were what caused the dispute. The lunch had taken place on a Saturday, and I was not informed about it. When he came home, I asked him whether he wanted lunch, and he said that he had eaten at work. I later found out from a friend that she had seen him at a local restaurant with someone that she did not recognize. After hearing this, I sent him a text message that asked, "Did you enjoy your lunch yesterday?"

He replied, "Gotta eat. It was free."

Although I had tried for over two decades to teach him to respond in ways that would decrease as opposed to increase my anger, it did not appear that he had learned anything.

"Take responsibility," I would say. "Don't minimize or justify your behaviors."

Yet once again, instead of saying, "I'm sorry I didn't tell you about it," his reply indicated that I should be fine with his lunch date, because food was a necessity and it hadn't cost him any money because she had bought.

Not only did poor Carlos have to experience temperatures outside that were sixty degrees below the lowest he had ever felt in his own country, he also often had to experience the frigidity inside our own household. Lee and I were pros at treating one another coldly, and I had perfected selective mutism. A chilly, speechless home was what sheltered Carlos for several days. He knew something was wrong, so I apologized and explained to him that Lee and I were having some difficulties in our marriage, at which he looked me straight in the eyes and said, "I think Lee very much love you. I wish you get happy."

It wasn't long after that when we reentered the good season during which Carlos, with Tyler beside him, opened the door to the garage to find us making out in the car.

"What you guys are doing in there?" Carlos asked.

We smiled, and they went back in the house.

When Carlos returned to Brazil in July 2007, I told him he was a good son. He had survived the four seasons of Iowa and the four seasons of our marriage.

CHAPTER
Fifty-Seven

In Missouri, I had been blessed with Trixie and the Trust Group, and in Iowa, my life was graced with LOLA. We were a small group of women who considered ourselves Ladies of Leisure and Adventure. We knew how to lounge by a pool and run from a bar fight. We loved to travel, shop, eat, and discuss our marriages; none of which were perfect. These were the ladies I turned to for comfort, acceptance, and laughter during the seasons of disaster.

We had our own set of LOLA rules that grew and changed, based on whatever activity we were engaged in: Rule #1—Chicks before Dicks; Rule #8—a LOLA does not make a derogatory comment about herself; Rule #16—LOLAs pose for pictures even if they have no makeup on; Rule #21—LOLAs take the stairs unless they are carrying too much wine; Rule #33—a LOLA should have a secret talent, such as putting her feet behind her head, standing on her head, or performing a special dance that includes flashlights or ribbons; Rule #38—no LOLA will ever be left behind; Rule #41—LOLAs who delete pictures from another LOLA's camera run the risk of being punched in the ovaries; Rule #45—if you see a LOLA across the street, you must yell, "Hello,

Lola," and run to her, being cautious to avoid moving cars or golf carts; Rule #55—if a LOLA needs to stop for Starbucks, DSW, or the bathroom, the stop is made without question; Rule #66—a LOLA does not say sorry unless a true offense has occurred; Rule #75—all rules are subject to change and are open to interpretation.

Occasionally our husbands were fortunate enough to engage in LOLA fun with us. In fact, Lee had earned the name *LTM*, otherwise known as Lee the Token Male. While other husbands found our escapades of girl love annoying and odd, Lee found us entertaining; therefore, he was willing to act as designated driver if we wanted to be together and have a little bit to drink.

One night, Lila, Baby Cakes—names chosen by them—and I went to a bar where Baby Cakes had promised to meet a friend. Lee was invited along as our DD, which he gladly complied with. I don't recall drinking to excess, but we did get silly. I looked down during the evening to see Lila crawling seductively toward us, imitating the dance done by the young girl in *Little Miss Sunshine*, our favorite movie. Baby Cakes and I roared with laughter, and Lila's behavior set the tone for over the top foolishness for the night.

Lee took several pictures of us hugging one another with such fierceness that our faces became distorted. He also took pictures of our swollen feet and close-ups of the inside of our elbows which turned out to look exactly like a butt. When we left at eleven-thirty, some people in the bar may have been glad to see us go.

We had gone less than a couple of miles on the darkened, deserted country road when I turned up the radio full blast and demanded that Lee stop the car, whereupon the LOLAs jumped out to dance. The headlights showcased our brilliant moves while Fergie sang, "G-L-A-M-O-R-O-U-S, yeah." Lee got out and joined us, and the four of us had a midnight dance party under the moon and the stars. We were flapping our arms, shaking our backsides, and jumping up and down while singing.

It was the sort of classic, fabulous fun that we LOLAs adored. We all knew one another's stories, and accepted one another for who we were. And in this case, this included Lee.

A couple of weeks later, I met the girls for dinner to vent about another bad choice Lee had made. During the meal, I asked, "Who would put up with all that I have put up with?" to which Lila and Baby Cakes replied in unison, "Jesus would."

LOLA's Rule #27-LOLAs advocate for one another's marriages.

CHAPTER

Fifty-Eight

When the LOLAs weren't around, I lived as if God and Jesus were my imaginary friends, often talking to them throughout my day. "Should I wear this top, Jesus? Or does it make me look a little slutty?" "Hey, God, I know I'm grouchy and judging others. I'll try to do better tomorrow." When driving in my car, I naturally assumed that Jesus was in the passenger seat beside me, and God was a backseat driver, constantly alert, giving directions, and ready to take over if necessary. We sometimes joked and laughed as I was on my way to or from work.

In February of 2008, I started working as a licensed mental health counselor. During the course of the job, I found myself providing a significant amount of marriage counseling and individual counseling for depression and anxiety. I wore a ring that had a cross on it, and during sessions, I would rub it and silently ask God to give me the right words. One day a session ran late because my last client asked me to pray with her, and I was a few minutes late heading home. Lee and I had plans to go to dinner with his parents, who were visiting, so he called my cell phone and asked, "Where are you? We're starving."

"You know me," I retorted. "I just thought I'd lollygag at work for a while," and then when I hung up, I asked aloud in the car, "Does he *not* know I'm doing the work of the Lord?"

And then we laughed, God, Jesus, and me, because that was a good one. God had to point out, though, that I had been a little unnecessarily sarcastic. Between him and the LOLAs, I never got a break. But that was okay. That was the way I liked it. I wanted to be challenged to be my best self.

I often told my clients in couples' counseling a story about a woman who told her lawyer that she wanted a divorce because of her husband's cruelty. The attorney said that he would be happy to draw up the paperwork; however, it was going to be a slow process and take a few months. The woman responded by asking him if he had any ideas of how she could get revenge on her husband in the meantime.

"Go home and treat him like a king," the attorney said. "Do all the things he loves, such as cook his favorite meals, rub his feet, and praise him. Then when the paperwork is complete, he will be completely content, and you can dump him." The woman left the office and did exactly as the attorney suggested. When the paperwork was complete, she returned, but only to say that she no longer needed it. She and her husband were leaving on a trip together. As soon as she began treating him like a king, he began to treat her like a queen.

With the aid of my friends, I would work to treat Lee like royalty and go easy on the sarcasm. This time, when I told him I was sorry that I had been short with him on the telephone, I was rewarded with a kiss.

CHAPTER

Fifty-Nine

Our marriage was like a game of Russian roulette, played with a gun that had hundreds of chambers. On the days that the chamber was empty we apologized easily, we communicated well, it was easy to hear God, and easy to trust. A happy day might look like this:

Sunday, 7:00 a.m.—we're still sleeping. I lie on my back with my leg draped over him.

7:15 a.m.—he stretches, gets up, and goes to the bathroom, and then crawls back in close to me. I roll toward him, snuggle up to him, and slide my hand around his waist and say, "I'm waking up with the world's greatest lover." He asks, "Did someone else crawl in with us during the night?"

We decide to spend a few more minutes in bed discussing what we love about one another. Lee says to me, "Don't just concentrate on my physical attributes." I laugh, and he says, "What's so funny?"

8:10 a.m.—we take Petey to the park and have a contest to see who can make the perfect Frisbee throw so that Handsome Pete can catch it.

8:45 a.m.—we make a ham and cheese omelet and share it.

9:30 a.m.—we take a shower together and then get ready for church.

11 a.m.—we attend mass with one or more of our children, depending on who is home. We race to be the first to open our song book to the right page, sing, and hold hands throughout the service. Lee doesn't fall asleep on a happy day.

12:15 p.m.—we return home. Tyler goes to a friend's house, and we change into comfortable clothes, have something simple for lunch, and then Lee relaxes on the couch with his feet propped up on the footstool, doing a little work on his computer while pausing once in a while to watch a football game on television. I nuzzle up to him and trace the outline of his ear with my tongue.

"Do you know what today's date is?" he asks, continuing to work.

I softly whisper into his ear. "I think it's the lickteenth."

"No, it's not the lickteenth," he says resolutely.

I nibble on his earlobe, and then press it between my lips before I question quietly, "Is it the suckteenth?"

He continues focusing on the screen, but nods in the affirmative as he says, "Yes, it is the suckteenth." I giggle as I move on top of him, pushing the computer off to the side.

2:00 p.m.—we watch football. He reads, and I write. We take a nap.

3:30 p.m.—I give him a much needed haircut, and when I nick his ear, and he complains, I say, "You always have the option of paying a professional to do this."

4:30 p.m.—he starts the grill for steaks and salmon. We work together to prepare potatoes, baked beans, and biscuits. While we are waiting for all the food to cook, we sit on the deck with a glass of wine and share an appetizer of dip and veggies.

5:45 p.m.—we eat. On the happiest of days, our three children are with us, and we hold hands around the dining room table and pray for God to bless our meal. While eating, we play a game. One of us comes up with a line from a movie, and everyone else tries to guess what movie it is.

Nicole says, "Once my good opinion is lost, it is lost forever."

"*Pride and Prejudice*," I say quickly, even though no one else would have gotten it.

"How about this one?" Lee asks. "'How dare you break wind before me?'"

Tyler responds with his best Austin Powers imitation, "Sorry, baby, I didn't know it was your turn."

We laugh. Renee throws out the next challenge. "If I'm a bird, you're a bird," and since it's from a movie she's watched about a hundred times, we all drone, "*The Notebook*."

I finish a bite of steak and scrape some more salmon onto my plate as I say, "I'm just a girl, standing in front of a boy, asking him to love her," and look hopefully at Lee.

"Don't tell me," he says, taking another bite of biscuit. "It's Hugh Grant and Julia Roberts in *Notting Hill*, right?"

"Good job, sweetie," I say and give him a kiss, which makes Tyler say, "Ew!"

Once everyone is done, we clean up together.

6:45 p.m.—Lee and I go to the video store to pick out a movie to curl up and watch.

7:00 p.m.—we return home with a new release, and we enjoy the movie, snuggled under a blanket together.

9:15 p.m.—we practice for the wife-carrying competition that we had seen on television. I stand on the footstool facing him, and he bends down and puts his head between my legs. I lean over and rest my chest on his back and wrap my arms around his waist. He stands up straight, and I am dangling upside down, my legs wrapped around his neck. The kids watch, amused, as we run circles around the house until I believe my head is going to explode.

"Stop," I say, "my head can't take it. It's a lot harder than it looks."

"I think you'd probably get used to it if we practiced more often."

"No, honey, I think we're going to have to take the wife-carrying competition off of our bucket list."

We agree to give up on our dream of the WCC.

9:30 p.m.—we tell the kids good night and go upstairs and get ready for bed. We floss together, and he climbs in bed to warm it up while I finish taking off my makeup.

10:00 p.m.—if he's not already asleep by the time I crawl in, we talk, and I wrap myself around him, intertwining my legs with his.

If I'm feeling feisty, which I usually am on happy days, I might jump on top of him and try to build a road on his chest by drumming my pointer fingers on his breast bone. That lasts merely seconds before he easily throws me off of him and pins me down on my back. I wiggle to get away but am no match for his strength, so I eventually give up and lay motionless under him saying, "Get off me."

"All right," he replies as he moves back on his side of the bed, "but stop bugging me and let me get some sleep."

"Is that really what you want?" I question, as I run my hand under the covers. "You really want me to stop bugging you?"

"Well…maybe you can bug me a little bit longer."

"You're pitiful," I say.

"You're the one who started it," he says.

At that point, we might make love, fall asleep, or pray together. All of which are good. Better than good.

CHAPTER

Sixty

And then, again without warning, the bullet appears that rips through the heart of happy. One Saturday night in the fall of 2008, Lee didn't come home until two in the morning. We had been distant and irritable with one another for the previous couple of days, but not for any particular reason other than the general stress of life. So when he left at five in the afternoon to play poker with some guys at one of their houses, I wasn't concerned. In fact, I looked forward to having an evening to myself since none of the children were going to be home. Having picked up some Chinese food, I watched *Pride and Prejudice* for the fiftieth time, straightened up the house, and then curled up in bed with Elizabeth Gilbert's *Eat, Pray, Love*, a story about how a woman recovers from a painful divorce. The further I read, the more I noticed in myself a sense of generalized frustration toward divorced people. *Weren't we supposed to marry for life and make it work?* Yet, at the same time, I was jealous of her. She had done something I had been unable to do. I didn't really want to be divorced, yet I envied her. Sometime between ten thirty and eleven, I fell asleep.

When I awoke at one thirty and realized that Lee was not home, I began to experience the familiar symptoms that characterized the malaise of our marital disorder, my mind running on fast legs to the past. Lee's poker games had never lasted this long before. My heart started to race, and I began to shake. It was two before I finally heard the garage door, and ten minutes later, the sound of the television turned on low.

I found him in the kitchen with his phone in his hand.

"What's going on?" I demanded. "Who are you talking to at this time of night?"

"Oh—um...I was just sending Scott a message that I made it home okay."

"Really? Since when do you guys check in with each other when you get home?"

Making no response, he sat down in front of the television and began to munch on the Taco Bell nachos that he had picked up.

"I thought Scott was going to have food at his house," I said.

"I was still hungry," he responded, making eye contact only with the television.

I took it easy on him and went back to bed.

He knew enough to sleep on the couch.

The next morning I awoke before him after a fitful sleep. Creeping downstairs, I checked his phone. All text messages had been deleted. The outgoing call log showed that he had called his friend, Brad, at twelve-fifteen.

I took the dog for a walk. As Petey and I were coming back from the park, Lee met us. We walked in strained silence for a couple of minutes before he said, "I was wide awake when poker ended, so I stopped at the Tilted Kilt for a drink before coming home. I'm sorry."

I considered my possible responses. I had been working hard on not resorting to my customary "Screw you!" so I decided on, "That's not okay," delivered without raising my voice. "You should not be hanging out by yourself until two in the morning in some sleazy bar where chicks are walking around with their tits hanging out."

"I know it's not okay," he told me. "That's why I'm apologizing."

"And that's supposed to make it all better?"

"Look. I said I'm sorry. All right? I don't know what else you want me to say."

I climbed our porch steps and planted myself in the rocking chair. "I don't know what I want you to say either. I'm sick to my stomach once again, because you care only about yourself and not about what is right for our relationship."

"You haven't wanted to be close to me for days," he said. "I didn't think you cared what I did."

"After all that we've been through and all that I've forgiven, you really don't think I care what you do?" My voice was growing louder.

"Oh, here we go again!" he exclaimed, throwing up his arms. "This is all about what I did over a decade ago. You know, you need to get some help and talk to a counselor."

I raised my eyebrows and looked right at him. "*I* need to talk to a counselor? *Really?* You think I'm the one who needs to go talk to somebody and get help?"

He turned and went into the house, leaving me to pump the rocking chair back and forth until he returned to repeat the fact that he was sorry.

"No," I said. "I do need someone to talk to, because I need to figure out why the hell I keep putting up with your crap. I'll call someone tomorrow."

We left it at that, but I could not stop obsessing about the text messages he had deleted. *Who had he been talking to late Saturday night?*

On Monday morning after he left for work, I pulled the file for bills from the desk drawer in the kitchen. I flipped through the papers until I found a recent statement, which provided me with the list of calls made from his number. As I scanned it, I began to feel physically ill, because my marriage was over. When Tyler came into the kitchen to have breakfast before leaving for school, I gave him an extra-long, extra-tight hug.

Once he was gone and Petey and I were the only two left in the house, I got out my planner. I compared the phone calls to the dates on my calendar. There were calls when I was gone to my family reunion, calls when he was in Chicago, and calls when I was out of town with my friends. And the calls, made between first thing in the morning and late at night had all been to a friend of mine named Barbara.

I called him at work and told him in no uncertain terms that I wanted him out of the house immediately.

"Julie, are you serious?" he exclaimed. "Just because I stopped at the bar the other night?"

"I'm not talking about that, you idiot," I told him. "I'm talking about the five hundred phone calls you placed to Barb when I was out of town. You're an asshole, and you need to come home and get your things out of this house." Then I hung up.

He called me back, but I answered and hung up again.

I took the dog to a vet appointment and when I returned, Lee was home.

Shoving the phone statement in his face, I preceded to scream and swear at him. And when he reached out for me, I told him not to touch me.

"Don't come anywhere near me!" I said, knowing that, if he came too close, I would start swinging, and the scene would become even uglier than it already was.

He said something about me making a big deal out of nothing. He said something about checking on my friend, because he knew she was going through a hard time. He said he didn't tell me because he knew I would overreact. His words were not soothing.

"Get the hell out," I told him. "Just get the hell out."

"I'm not leaving," he told me. "We can work through this. It's not that big of a deal."

"Fine," I said. "If you won't leave, I will."

I called my friend Jen, and she said I could stay with her. I also called an emergency LOLA meeting. My marriage was sinking in quicksand, but I knew enough to be thankful and reach out for my support. I had great friends, a good job, and excellent health.

Probably the most painful part of all of this was telling the children. I called Nicole, who was now teaching ninth grade English in North Carolina. She handled it well, probably because she may have been fairly confident that we would work through it, because we had worked through so much in the past. When I called Renee, who was a junior at the University of Iowa, she said that she was sad but that she understood and would support me no matter what ended up happening. She too had some idea that I had already forgiven much. Tyler, who was now a sophomore in high school, made very little response, but I found out later that he had called Nicole and had asked her what he should do.

As for Lee, he continued to tell me that I was blowing the situation way out of proportion. He insisted that he was innocent of everything except staying out late in a bar and making a few calls to Barb. He'd throw in a *sorry* here or there, but they were usually lame and followed with a *but*: "but you make such a big deal out of everything," "but I can never talk to you, because you get so angry," and "but you aren't perfect either."

On the way to my girlfriend's house, I called him. "This is extremely humiliating and embarrassing for me, and I can't believe our life has turned out like this."

"You're the one who chose to leave," he said. "We should be able to stay together and work through this without you running away."

"You mean I should just forgive and move on once again," I said. "Forget that you have broken every promise you've ever made to me, and forget that, every time I've been out of town, you've secretly reached out to a friend of mine. That would be convenient for you, wouldn't it? As usual, you don't get the severity of what you've done. Talking to you does nothing to help me feel better, so I need to get off the phone now."

Once comfortably settled in Jen's guest bedroom, I asked myself if I was overreacting. I remembered again my ninth-grade boyfriend who had been talking on the phone regularly to my best friend behind my back. I had broken up with him. It was twenty-five years later, and I still felt like I was dealing with high school drama, but this time it wasn't as simple as giving back a class ring wrapped with angora string.

A couple of days later, when Lee told me that I could come back home, and he would move out, I said okay. There were times when what he said and did made sense and he appeared to understand that he had pushed our relationship too far. But then, when I continued holding onto the anger, he would lash out, telling me that I was controlling and verbally abusive. He defended himself by saying that he was just a friendly guy, and I needed to stop trying to control him and put restrictions on him. He said he should be able to go to bars if he wanted, drink as much as he wanted, and talk to whomever he wanted. It was not a convincing argument. I let him move out and into a friend's home, and I slipped back into my own, cold bed.

I began participating in individual counseling, as did Lee, and we began seeing someone as a couple. I couldn't remember how many counselors there had been before her, but she could hear and see and didn't want to talk to me about my father, so that was refreshing. In our first couples' session in the small, cozy room with blue walls, Lee did most of the talking. He spoke with nervous speed and played with his wedding band while recounting the vast history of our bipolar marriage. I watched on as he chattered from his cushy, swivel chair and twisted his ring round and round. About halfway through the session, the ring came off. He stopped midsentence and said to the therapist, "Hang on. I've dropped my wedding ring." He looked at the floor, the cushion, and ran his hand down the sides of the chair. He moved the chair to see under it, and then he picked it up and shook it. Nothing; his wedding ring had disappeared.

"That's not a good sign," he said, looking back and forth between the counselor and me.

"No, it's not," I replied.

We finished the session, and the counselor agreed to call if she found the ring, after which Lee and I went our separate ways. On that damp and dreary day, as I pulled out of the parking ramp, I saw him walking back to work with his head down. Turning in the other direction, I went home. He had been careless with his wedding ring, just as he had been with our marriage.

CHAPTER

Sixty-One

Believe it or not, I still did not really want to get divorced. It was true that the freedom of being single was somewhat appealing, and I spent a good deal of time designing my own condo in my mind, but I couldn't reconcile myself to give up the really good times. Yet I also did not want to live in fear every day of what Lee might be doing behind my back. And he seemed unable to gauge what was appropriate behavior and what was not.

I told Nicole and Renee that I did not want a divorce. I wanted their father to give me some indication that he understood the unhealthiness of his behaviors and that he wanted to respect me and our relationship without minimizing what I needed to feel safe and secure. I shared with the girls that instead of reassuring me, he presented me with platitudes like, "It doesn't do any good to worry," and "Life is too short to be unhappy." Instead of taking responsibility, he engaged in hyperbole: "I'm just a horrible person. I don't deserve to live." Instead of sincerely expressing a desire to change, he would say, "I don't plan to do those things anymore." He would swing from looking up $200 divorces on the Internet and telling me we were done, to begging me to stay. I would swing from thinking divorce was not right to thinking divorce was the only way.

About three weeks into our separation, he had come over to talk with me while no one else was home. We talked about him going to the bars, and he said he would not do that again. We talked about the calls, and he reemphasized that they were innocent, a claim that I knew was true after having talked to Barb. We discussed the past, and he said that he would never make the same bad choices again. It wasn't exactly a word miracle, because I think he had made most of these promises before, but I thought it was going well. I was feeling better. He seemed sincere.

"But don't you think you need to take some responsibility," he asked, "because marriage is a two-way street? And you're not perfect, you know."

My inner fault line created an immediate bodyquake of ten points on the Richter scale. "What?" I exploded. "Are you kidding me? You want me to take responsibility for my part in screwing up this marriage!"

My instinct was to slap him, but I didn't want this confrontation to become physical, so I hurried into the entryway and then up the stairs, screaming, "We need to be done! You are unbelievable!"

"So you're just going to give up!" he shouted back at me. "You're really going to do that to our kids? You're going to destroy their family?"

Any ounce of sanity that I might have had left deserted me when he said that.

"How much more do I have to forgive in order to prove my love for my children?" I demanded. "Is there no end? If I truly loved them, then I would forgive, and we would move on one more time. Is that it? Fine!"

And then, pulling off my T-shirt and bra and hurling them down at him, I cried, "Let's go! Let's screw and make up, if that's what's required of a good and loving mother, because no one, no one loves their children more than me!"

At that point, I paused to slip out of my jeans and my underwear. He stared up at me unsure of what to do. The devil was pleased that I had finally lost control, and I believe he was urging Lee to lose control as well. He began to remove his shirt.

"Come on!" I yelled, tears streaming down my cheeks. "We'll have sex, and we will be friends again. I will show God and my children that I will forgive infidelity, drinking, and lying, and just keep on screwing on. I will forgive anything!"

At that, Lee pulled his shirt back down and started up the stairs. I headed into the bathroom, screaming, "I hate you! I hate you for what you have done to me and this family! It's unforgivable!"

Before I could lock the door, he came in. Strangely enough, he seemed perfectly calm, but his eyes were sad.

"Close your eyes!" I told him. "Close your eyes and picture me having sex with someone else. And then picture me enjoying it, because that's what I've had to picture for all these years!"

I let him hold me then, dampening the front of his shirt with my tears. "I hate you," I said once again, barely more than a whisper.

After asking him to leave, which he eventually did reluctantly, I turned the water to hot and stepped in. As I stood in the shower, the slide show ran through my head: my husband sleeping with other women, my husband drunk and mean, my husband flirting and gawking and making secret phone calls. It had been twelve years since Lee told me about his unfaithfulness and here I stood, wanting to start hitting my head repeatedly against the shower walls until the slides were knocked out of the projector in my mind so I never had to see them again. Instead I stood directly under the showerhead and let the scalding water wash over me. I closed my eyes and imagined the memories being burned away.

I stepped out of the shower exhausted and, curling up on the closet floor, wept until I had nothing left.

CHAPTER

Sixty-Two

"Be still and know that I am God" (Psalm 46:10, NIV). That was the verse God spoke to me. I had been melodramatic on the previous day, and now, feeling mildly ashamed of myself, and assuming that God had been somewhat unsettled as well, I made the decision to take myself on a retreat to a nearby spirituality center. Or maybe God encouraged me to make the decision. I'm not sure.

Even though the center was within a few miles of my home, I had only ventured onto the grounds once several years before to attend a brief lecture. Situated on seventy acres of prairies and woodlands, it was meant to be a place of solitude and reflection. On the early Sunday afternoon, as I pulled onto the property, I immediately regretted that I had not sought comfort here sooner. Somehow, I felt completely protected from the outside world, as though enclosed by invisible walls. As I drove up to the retreat center, a space devoted to ecology and spirituality, I didn't know what to expect. But I was certain that I would not be disappointed. The air smelled of damp leaves and firewood, and the prairie grasses stretched away on every side, dotted with oak trees that were already changing color.

Asking God to lead the way, I started toward the north edge of the woods where I suspected a trail head might be. My suspicions were correct. My shoes crunched the leaves and brush as I entered the worn pathway. I had walked hardly any distance at all before I chanced upon a Labyrinth. A single layer of bricks outlined the circular course that had a diameter of about twenty feet. According to a plaque attached to a post, if I walked the meandering path to the center, it was supposed to lead me to a meditative, problem-evaporating state of mind.

I did not wish to enter it immediately. I needed time to prepare, time to process my thoughts before trying to empty my mind. I sat on a log bench positioned near the starting point of the labyrinth, reflecting upon my situation, occasionally being distracted by my surroundings—the birds that chirped above my head and the grasses that tickled my legs. There was a dark wooden cross positioned beside the trail, wrapped loosely in barbed wire, and I pictured myself kneeling before it, weeping tears of remorse like the sinner I was.

My circumstances were, I knew, all too familiar; the story of a promise broken, a selfish man who dabbled in Christianity, and a woman at once intolerant and overly benevolent who wanted to love God above all else. Change, as I saw it, was utterly unobtainable, yet agonizingly desirable. *Could I*, I wondered, *find the answers in the labyrinth?* Before ringing the heavy metal bell that would signal the beginning of my journey, I glanced once more at the cross and invited Jesus to accompany me. And then, one sandal step after another, I hesitantly trod the clearly marked path, telling God that I had been self-centered and angry. *One foot after another. I don't know if I can stay married. But I believe that is what you want of me. Please guide me.*

And as I walked slowly on, and found center, I heard, *You need only trust me. You need only trust in me.* And with that I felt a peace like I had never felt before, because I realized my happiness resided in my relationship with God regardless of whether I was with Lee or not. I wanted answers, and God made me aware that He is the answer to all my questions.

CHAPTER
Sixty-Three

Labor Day 2009: nearly a year had passed since I had walked the Labyrinth. Irish dancers were performing on the television during the Muscular Dystrophy Telethon, and my mind wandered to a couple that I had counseled the previous week. The husband had been unfaithful to his wife, and I had shared my own struggles, as I sometimes did, in an effort to give hope to those who didn't want to give up but thought they had to. The distraught wife said, "No offense, but I've always looked down on women like you and Hillary Clinton—women who stay with men who have cheated."

"I'm not offended," I replied. "It doesn't bother me for you to say that, because I'm happy. At the end of the day, I will go home, and my husband and I will laugh, and we will play, and we will be with our children, and we will be a family. I gave my children a gift by staying, and ultimately, it turned out to be a gift to myself. I will never regret that, no matter what the future brings and no matter what others think of me."

Remembering those words, I snuggled up even closer to Lee and smiled at those dancers on the television. Before driving away from the spirituality center the previous fall, I had called him and told him that he could move back into our home. I still expected him to make changes and work harder for our marriage, and I knew the marriage would continue to be challenging, but as long as my relationship with God was healthy, I could handle the difficulties that would come.

CHAPTER

Sixty-Four

Lee was insistent that he needed to leave to get my birthday present. The morning of my forty-third birthday, October 6, 2009, had arrived, and it was a Sunday. Few stores were open on a Sunday morning, so I suspected that he would be shopping at Walmart. Since gifts are not my love language, I would have rather he'd stayed home, fixed a big breakfast, and spent time with me. But he looked so excited that I knew he wanted to buy something that he thought I just had to have.

"Couldn't you have bought it earlier?" I grumbled, but he was already gone, and besides, I was only pretending to be upset. Tyler wouldn't be up for another hour, and the peace and quiet was a welcome reprieve. However, when over two hours passed and Lee had not returned, I became slightly annoyed because I had hoped we could spend the day together. I asked Tyler if he knew what his father was going to buy for me, but he pleaded ignorance, and he wasn't hard to believe. Tyler was a great teenager, but his short-term memory was defective and, unless a person was speaking to him about girls, cars, or electronics, he wasn't going to remember the conversation, which meant, in this case, I could rule out a BMW and a big screen television as my potential presents.

When I heard the garage door go up, I prepared myself to be enthusiastic, no matter what. Previous gifts had ranged from a disappointing lawn mower to the surprisingly beautiful diamond anniversary band, although most had been smaller and food related: a chocolate chip cookie cake, a box of chocolates, and an entire black tie mousse cake from the Olive Garden.

Lee had said many times, "The quickest way to your heart is through your stomach." But when he came into the kitchen, wearing a cocky grin, he was empty-handed.

"Do you want your present now or later?" he asked.

"Well, I've already been waiting for two hours," I teased him, "I suppose I could wait a little longer."

"But you won't," he told me, and dashed back out to the car, reappearing in a minute with our daughter, Renee, in his arms.

Lee, it seemed, had driven all the way to the University of Iowa to bring our daughter home to spend the day with me.

"You're the best present I've ever gotten," I said to her with great certainty, before hugging her tightly.

We watched a movie, ate Chinese food, and then played Rock Band on the Xbox 360. Tyler chose to play the guitar. He leaned back on the bar stool he had brought in from the kitchen, had one leg out straight, the other bent with his foot resting on the rung of the chair, and the guitar draped lazily across his body.

As for me, I drummed the colored circles of the game, hair loose and mussed up, in character. And Lee was our vocalist with ball cap turned sideways and microphone resting on his chin while Renee volunteered to be our backup dancer.

We performed "Rock You Like a Hurricane," and we were better than any rock group that had come before us. Okay, maybe we weren't that good, but I was happier than a rock star, glad that I had stayed in my marriage, and glad that I had fought to forgive.

That night, as we lay spooning in bed, Renee came in to kiss us good night.

"Hey, Renee," Lee said, "if your mom and I die together, will you have us buried like this, because the only way I'm going to get to heaven is if I'm hanging onto your mom."

We laughed. There had been a time when that might have been the case; however, over the years of our marriage, Lee had developed his own relationship with God, and because our God is a forgiving God, I knew Lee could make it into heaven of his own accord. At his core, Lee was someone who would help a person in need, give a smile to a stranger, and drop whatever he might be doing if one of his children asked something of him. He was and is a sinner, as am I, but Jesus is the friend of sinners, and therefore, Lee will be invited to the heavenly concert when the end comes, regardless of me.

As Renee left the room, I lay there, listening to him as the changes in his breathing indicated that he was quickly falling asleep and then made the sign of the cross and whispered, "Thank you, God, for loving your children. Thank you."

CHAPTER

Sixty-five

At the beginning of the year 2010, a very dear friend had e-mailed me the following passage:

> It is a mistake to be always turning back to recover the past. The law for Christian living is not backward, but forward; not for experiences that lie behind, but for doing the will of God, which is always ahead and beckoning us to follow. Leave the things that are behind, and reach forward to those that are before, for on each new height to which we attain, there are the appropriate joys that befit the new experience. Don't fret because life's joys are fled. There are more in front. Look up, press forward, the best is yet to be!
>
> —F.B. Meyer in "Our Daily Walk,"
> *Christianity Today*, Vol. 40. No 1.

I took that to heart, posted it on my refrigerator, and referred to it when the hurts from the past tried their hardest to drive me to obsession. I also focused on it when my selfish self wanted to remind Lee of all the bad choices he had made in our marriage.

And I looked at it eleven months later as we headed out the door to stay a night in Galena, Illinois, to celebrate our silver anniversary.

We hadn't planned an extravagant trip, even though we both felt it was a special occasion, combining it instead with a short business trip that Lee had to make to Galena. The Irish Cottage Boutique Hotel, at which he had booked a room, looked a bit garish from the outside, particularly since the vibrant red, orange, blue, and green exterior indicated that it was a far cry from the quaint bed and breakfast I had been expecting. However, my maternal grandparents had immigrated to America from Ireland, so I enjoyed a connection to anything Irish and tried to stay open-minded.

As soon as we stepped foot in the lobby, I knew that I was wrong to have questioned, even silently, Lee's choice of a place to stay. The dark mahogany and rich oak woodwork along with the brown leather chairs, loveseats, and sofas created a luxurious setting, and the library drew me to it like a magnet. Hundreds of jacket-free hardback books lined the walls in every color of the rainbow: dull reds, vivid oranges, golden yellows, bright greens, pale blues, and bold purples, all begging to be opened and read. Above the wooden cabinets that neatly housed the rows of books were written the names of famous authors, such as C.S. Lewis, James Joyce, William Yeats, and George Bernard Shaw. As an aspiring writer, I was inspired yet intimidated. Regardless, I breathed in the scent of paper, leather, and wood, and resolved to press on with the work I felt called to do.

The rooms were named after Irish counties, and ours, County Downs, had a whirlpool tub and a king-size bed just as our honeymoon suite had twenty-five years before. I smiled a grin of remembrance and gave Lee a squeeze around the waist before we sat down to share the lunch that we had picked up.

After Lee left for a meeting, I arranged a table and chair in front of the window and sat down to write, certain that I would be inspired by the view. Only then did I notice the large cross set atop one of the rolling hills. *Had God*, I wondered, no doubt egotistically, *put it there especially for me?* I was certain of one thing, and that was that He had most assuredly brought us to this place. Gazing at that faraway symbol of everything forgiven, I felt an incredible sense of peacefulness. Time had brought me to a wonderful spot, and I wrote the following: "The sun sets, and the sun rises, and it doesn't care how much money or power you possess, because all of us, over the passage of time, will find ourselves powerless in the hands of God."

Thus far my life had passed in a blink. I had one quick chance to work toward being my best and giving my best. My marriage over the past couple of years had become stronger and felt safe. My children were healthy, happy, and well-adjusted. My job was fulfilling and flexible. Lulled by contentment, I napped only to awake to find the library calling. W.B. Yeats whispered, down the hall and under the door, an invitation, and I accepted. I joined the great writers of Ireland and found inspiration by simply turning the pages. But when Lee returned, they graciously went back to their place in history, and I took down a book entitled *The Art of Being Happily Married* by Maurois and Herbert. Flipping to the last chapter, entitled "The Silver Wedding," with Lee sitting snugly beside me on the sofa, I read aloud:

> Marise: Perhaps that's why you don't think me too stupid… For we have twenty-five years of mutual memories behind us! What a lot we've experienced together! War, births, deaths, friendship, failure and success…

> Philippe: And this fragile link that united us has held throughout it all.

> Marise: Just once it nearly broke…When you came back from Sweden in love with another woman…completely bewitched.

Philippe: Don't talk about that today, Marise. That's all dead and forgotten…

Marise: Oh, I often think of her, and I like to talk about her, now that it's over. After all, it was Dolores who strengthened the link between us. When I threatened to leave you and said you had to choose between her and me, you chose me. Then I realized that I really *did* mean something to you… And it was a lesson to me too. You see, I'd begun to let myself go. I took your love so much for granted that I no longer troubled about pleasing you or making you happy. Well, this affair of yours made me realize that marriage doesn't just run itself…. It's a match you have to play and win each day.

Philippe: And each night.

We laughed and gazed at one another through tear-filled eyes. The couple could have been the two of us, and the funniest part was that the book was written in 1953.

That night we shared a fabulous, intimate dinner. The next morning we put on our walking shoes and started off, in the crisp morning air, on a journey to the cross, beginning our hike at the open grassy area at the side of the hotel, which, according to the plaque nailed to the marker, was called a *fairie* ring. According to folklore, if you were lured into the ring by the dancing fairies; they would take years from your life.

"I'm willing to risk it," I told Lee.

At first he only watched as I skipped into the circle and did my own rendition of the chicken dance. But then I took his hands and led him into the circle saying, "Don't be afraid. The fairies won't hurt you."

"I don't want to be tricked," he responded, "I want a lot more years with you."

After dancing, we jogged down a gully and trudged up a long hill, and there it was—the symbol of my Savior's death. I wasn't quite sure what to do. Hug it? Stare at it? Sit by it?

After we took pictures of each of us standing by it and sent them to our children, we held hands and gave thanks for our life, our love, and our everything. There was nothing we weren't thankful for in that moment. I loved the whole world. We were choosing happy together.

That was a fabulous day. Our time in Galena was amazing. Bedroom day was even better.

I had asked to spend twenty-four hours in our bedroom at home on the day after we returned from our brief trip. Lee did not put up much of a fight. In the morning, we went outside long enough to take Pete for a quick walk that would hopefully calm him down for most of the day. Otherwise, he would have driven us crazy by bringing us random socks and dishtowels and whining by the bedside. After that, we ate breakfast in bed—omelets, strawberries with whipped cream, and mimosas—that we had prepared together, after which, we looked through our wedding album, lingering wistfully over the photographs of the young couple we had been, looking into one another's eyes, so genuinely in love, with no idea how difficult long-term, committed love would be. We reminisced about the honeymoon, the farmhouse, and the baby that had been born to us that first year, and I thought about the fact that I had no regrets.

After breakfast was cleared away, we assembled our massage table by the curtained window, lit candles, and turned on Jim Brickman. Lee gave me a wonderful hour-long rub down. Some might think that was generous of him, but believe me, it worked out to his favor.

At ten thirty, the serene spa became a *College Game Day* party room, and propping pillows up behind us, we chanted, "Let's go, Hawks!" And at halftime, with the Hawks behind, we turned our shirts around, but tragically, they ended up losing the game by four points. We let Prince perk us up by watching *Purple Rain*, the first movie we had ever seen together, and then at the end of what had been an amazing day, I took my wedding dress out of storage, and paraded in front of the children, thoroughly surprised when Renee said that she might want to wear it when she was married.

That night, when I lay back in bed, sated and sleepy, I thought over our quarter of a century together. Some people might think I was crazy for giving myself back over to him so completely, and I've definitely had times when *I* thought I was crazy. I've often felt that I was too good for this man and he did not deserve me. But I've come to realize that it is in those moments that I think myself superior that I cease to be significant at all.

I once wrote, "It must be hard for him to not be as wonderful as I." When I read over that line, I thought, *It must be hard for him to be married to someone who thinks themselves as wonderful as I.* He too had gone through so much to stay married. We both worked hard to save our family, and he truly would do most anything in the world for me. We still weren't perfect. Jealousy continued to be present at times, as well as anxiety and sometimes hurt, but the point was that with every fight, we learned more about each other, ourselves, and our relationship, and we knew that even if we never completely figured it out, in the end, the trying was worth it. I held no regrets.

I thought he was already asleep when he said, "I'm crazy about you, Jewel," and I replied, "I'm crazy about you too, babe."

"Then there's a pair of us."

"Yep, there's a pair of us," I said. "Don't tell. They'd banish us you know."

Our lives are not determined by what happens to us. Our lives are determined by how we handle what happens to us—

—Anonymous

Author's Note

Since finishing the book a couple of years ago, the marriage has continued to have its ups and downs. But my relationship with God has remained steadfast. It is that relationship that assists me in choosing happiness in my everyday life. God reminds me that I answer only for myself and only to Him. I've learned that if I'm not careful, the world can convince me that I am wrong to be with my husband. The world wants to give each of us opinions about any number of situations, and it can become easy to feel not good enough. So I choose to listen to God who tells me that He loves me. When I second-guess the marriage, He reminds me of the joyful times that I have experienced with my family and the playful times I have enjoyed with my husband as a result of staying. He hints at the joys to come should I remain His faithful servant. I wish God's blessings on all my readers whatever your struggles may be.